The Northern Yorkshire D[...]

C000156193

CONTENTS

WALKED AND WRITTEN BY CHARLIE EMETT & BILL BAMLETT.
SERIES CONCEPT AND DESIGN: MALCOLM PARKER.
ARTWORK AND DESIGN: RACHEL PAXTON & ANDREW FALLON.

PUBLISHED BY WALKS OF DISCOVERY LTD.,
1 MARKET PLACE, MIDDLETON-IN-TEESDALE,
CO. DURHAM, DL12 0QG. TEL: (01833) 640638.

PRINTED IN ENGLAND.
ISBN 0-86309-119-9.
COPYRIGHT © WALKS OF DISCOVERY LIMITED 1994.

F DIFFICULTY:
asy to Moderate
rate to Strenuous
remely Strenuous

IMPORTANT: Please note that these above gradings and the time lengths quoted below are based on the personal experience of the author and may vary significantly between individual walkers

How to use this Guide

This guide must only be used by the most serious of hill walkers who are fully prepared, equipped and experienced at walking in such demanding and difficult mountainous terrain.

■ **1** CHOOSE YOUR ROUTE Study the general location map opposite indicating our selection of 15 walk routes, then consult their individual route summary, background information, route description and route map before making your personal choice. Each 'circular' walk starts and finishes at the same point for your convenience.

■ **2** CHECK THE ROUTE SUITABILITY Carefully study your selected route to ensure that it is suitable for you, but particularly the weakest member of your party. To do this also consider the grading system for length and degree of difficulty for each route on the contents page - as well as the ascent, descent and cross-section information detailed on each individual walk description.

■ **3** CHECK THE WEATHER CONDITIONS Before you set out it is essential that you check the current and developing weather conditions. In addition, you should consider the Walking and Safety Tips on page 66. Also be aware of the telephone numbers of the emergency services.

■ **4** USE WITH AN ORDNANCE SURVEY MAP This guide is designed to be used with the relevant 1:25 000 scale O.S. Maps of the area. Grid references are used with the route descriptions in the guide.

■ **5** USING THE MAP AND ROUTE DESCRIPTION TOGETHER This guide is designed so that the route map and route description are on facing pages so that they may be viewed from one side of a map case, with the relevant 1:25 000 Ordnance Survey Map folded to the appropriate area viewed from the other side of the map case.

■ **6** USING THE ROUTE SECTIONS Each route is divided into a number of logical lettered sections which are clearly marked on the route map, in the route descriptions and on the cross-section. These should help you navigate your route.

■ **7** FOLLOWING THE ROUTE The detailed, concise route descriptions are clearly numbered in both the text and on the route map to help you locate your position.

■ **8** SHORT CUTS It is always best to plan for the unexpected and to be prepared for any eventuality. To assist you we have suggested some short cut alternatives should they be required.

Tourist Information

(NP) = National Park. (S) = Seasonal.
AYSGARTH FALLS (NP)
Tel: (01969) 663424
BARNARD CASTLE 43 Galgate.
Tel: (01833) 690909
BEDALE (S) - but open Tuesdays in winter. Bedale Hall.
Tel: (01677) 424604
BENTHAM (S) Station Road.
Tel: (015242) 62549
CLAPHAM (NP) (S)
Tel: (015242) 51419
GRASSINGTON (NP) (S) Colvend, Hebden Road.
Tel: (01756) 752774
HARROGATE Royal Baths Assembly Rooms, Crescent Rd.
Tel: (01423) 525666
HAWES (NP) (S) Dales Countryside Museum, Station Yard.
Tel: (01969) 667450
HAWORTH 2-4 West Lane.
Tel: (01535) 642329
HORTON-IN-RIBBLESDALE Pen-y-Ghent Cafe.
Tel: (01729) 860333
INGLETON (S) Community Centre Car Park, Main Street.
Tel: (015242) 41049
KIRKBY LONSDALE 24 Main Street.
Tel: (015242) 71437
KIRKBY STEPHEN Market Street.
Tel: (017683) 71199
KNARESBOROUGH (S) 35 Market Place.
Tel: (01423) 866886
LEYBURN Thornborough Hall.

Tel: (01969) 23069/22773
MALHAM (NP) Car Park.
Tel: (01729) 830363
REETH Swaledale Folk Museum, The Green.
Tel: (01748) 884373
RICHMOND Friary Gardens, Victoria Road.
Tel: (01748) 850252
RIPON (S) Minster Road.
Tel: (01765) 604625
SCOTCH CORNER (S) The Pavilion Services.
Tel: (01325) 377677
SEDBERGH (NP) (S) 72 Main Street.
Tel: (015396) 20125
SETTLE Open mornings only in winter months. Town Hall.
Tel: (01729) 825192

Useful Information

FELL RESCUE SERVICES
Contact the Police. Tel: 999
WEATHER FORECAST
Recorded information Tel: (0898) 500 417
LONG DISTANCE WALKERS ASSOCIATION
117 Higher Lane, Rainford, St Helens, Merseyside, WA11 8BQ.
Tel: (01744) 882638
DISCOVERY VISITOR CENTRE
1 Market Place, Middleton-in-Teesdale,
County Durham, DL12 0QG.
Tel & Fax: (01833) 640638 for details of current and forthcoming Walks of Discovery walking guides.

General Map of the Area
Showing the Walk Locations

N

© Crown Copyright

GENERAL KEY

Tourist Information		Picnic Site		Coniferous Woodland
National Park Centre		Caravan Site		Deciduous Woodland
Nature Reserve		Site of Fort		Mixed Woodland
Natural Attraction		Viewpoint		Built-up Area
Castle		Parking Area		Location Arrow
Historic Building		Public Toilets		Route direction
Cathedral/Church/Abbey		Location of summit		Route along road
Ancient Monument	643m	Height above sea-level		Short Cut/Escape Route

ABOVE 500m	Field Boundaries
350m – 500m	A Roads
200m – 350m	B Roads
BELOW 200m	Minor Roads
Lakes/Reservoirs	Service Roads/Tracks (Often Private Roads)
	Major Roundabout

MILES
KILOMETRES

KELD-RAVENSEAT-TAN HILL-STONESDALE-KELD CIRCULAR

10.5 MILES (16.8 km)

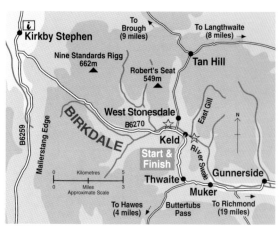

Route Details

Distance	10.5 miles (16.8 km)
Degree of Difficulty	Strenuous
Ascent	354m (1160ft)
Time	6 hours

Start and Finish Points

Keld is well sited at the head of Swaledale, where some of the dale's most spectacular scenery is found. It lies a little north of the B6270 at a point where the road curves westwards on approaching the River Swale, north of Kisdon. By road, its only access is either one of two short roads which meet to form two sides of a triangle, the third being the B6270 itself. Most of the hamlet's stout buildings huddle around a triangle of sloping tarmac, at the bottom right-hand corner of which a signpost directs you along a track. Here the walk begins and ends.

Maps Needed

OS Outdoor Leisure No 30 (1:25 000)

Parking Facilities

To reach Keld's small car park at Park Lodge, drive through to the bottom of the hamlet and then turn left. There is an honesty box at the entrance. As parking spaces are scarce in Keld, an early start is advisable. There are public toilets on entering Keld.

Short Cuts

The height, length and remoteness of the route makes it pointless trying to select specific emergency short cuts. In adverse or deteriorating weather, or other urgent situations, reaching the nearest public road or settlement may prove prudent.

Route Summary

From Keld, the route crosses the Swale and follows its course upstream almost to its confluence with Whitsundale Beck. It continues upstream, to descend to Ravenseat. From there it climbs out of Whitsun Dale, along Pryclose Gutter, edging Lock Gill, where the highest point of the walk is reached on the eastern flank of Robert's Seat. The descent along Robert's Seat Band is airy and exhilarating. It leads to Tongue Sike, beyond which Thomas Gill is edged on the descent to Stonesdale Beck.

Leaving Keld the countryside is extremely beautiful

The way ahead continues through wild moorland, and Tan Gill is edged before the West Stonesdale road is reached. A short walk, left, along this quiet road will bring you to a junction from where turn right to arrive at Tan Hill, England's highest inn. From Tan Hill, the way, along the edge of Stonesdale Moor, coincides with the Pennine Way almost to Keld. The route is well defined, and excellent to walk. The Swale is re-crossed and the far bank is climbed to a point where the Pennine Way begins to contour Kisdon and you turn right, along a track, to return to Keld, the start of this magnificent walk.

Interesting Features

GEOLOGY The moors around Tan Hill are pitted with dangerous abandoned shafts, so it is advisable to keep to the track southwards from the inn. This section is shared with the Pennine Way.

If you like juicy bits, then Lad Gill and its surroundings will be to your liking! The ground thereabouts is soggy even when it is bone dry everywhere else.

LANDFORMS From the farm track west of East Stonesdale, the views of the Swale below and on your left, are excellent and Keld is seen to advantage. From this vantage point the original course of the Swale is clearly seen as a dry valley, which goes to the west of Kisdon.

The U-shaped valley along which it now flows so spectacularly to the east of Kisdon tells of the tremendous glacial pressures brought to play as the river's new course was gouged.

Catrake Force cannot be seen from the route but East Gill Force, on leaving Keld, and Wain Wath Force, near the white limestone, tree fringed Cotterby Scar, can; and what a splendid sight they make, with the swift flowing waters spilling over them!

HISTORY Norsemen were the first people to settle in Upper Swaledale arriving in the 10th century. This exhilarating walk crosses geographical features and touches places with names that are Old Norse in origin, starting in Keld, which is derived from 'Keld' meaning spring.

Ravenseat is derived from the Norse 'Hrafn's Saetr'. The first name is personal and the second one, 'saetr' means shieling or hill pasture.

The narrow path running south-westwards from Tan Hill along the rim of Stonesdale Moor and past Robert's Seat House to descend to Ravenseat, was once a jagger or packhorse road along which coal was carried from Tan Hill mines.

Tan Hill, at 528m (1732ft), is England's highest inn. Coal was being mined there as early as the 14th century. By the mid-17th century when Lady Anne Clifford was heating Appleby Castle with Tan Hill coal, the beginnings of mechanisation were evident.

'They have also engines that draw up their coal in sort of baskets in a well', Celia Fennes observed. It was not until the 18th century that an inn was built at Tan Hill. However, as though in atonement for 400 years of miners for whom it had come too late, the builders constructed it in triplicate. The main structure was an inn and two more inns were built in outbuildings. The place was first named King's Pit House after King's Pit, one of the mine shafts. Later it was renamed Tan Hill after Tan Hill Pit, another mine shaft, and Tan Hill it remains to this day.

Susan Peacock lived at Tan Hill from 1902 until her death on 24th May, 1937. An inscription to her memory is cut into a rocky outcrop at the rear of the building.

The picturesque East Gill Force where it enters the River Swale

PEOPLE Standing proud and above Keld is a solitary building with a gloriously happy past, the Cat Hole Inn. The ale was good, all the food was home-made, the ham was home cured from home raised pigs, and the speciality of the house was ham and eggs. Throughout Christendom there were no ham and egg meals to compare for flavour and goodness than those cooked by Agnes Hutchinson of the Cat Hole. They were famous.

Roughly midway between Smithy Holme and the rim of How Edge Scars and to the right of your line of walk there is a sheepfold, Eddyfold, that for sheer size takes some beating. On seeing it, Wainwright pronounced that it was the biggest sheepfold he had ever seen.

Cross-Section of the Route

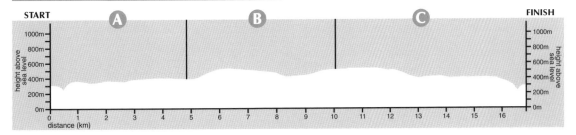

Route Description

SECTION A	2.5 Miles (4 Km)		
Destination	Ravenseat (GR 863034)		
Ascent	90m(295ft)	Descent	24m(79ft)

■ **1** From the north-east corner of Keld, below the cemetery, go along the walled track signposted to Muker and where, on joining the Pennine Way, the path bifurcates, go left, downhill, and through a gate to the River Swale, which you cross on a footbridge. Continue along a clear path, climbing slightly left and passing East Gill Force on your right, above which, where a track signposted Coast to Coast crosses your line of walk, turn left along it to climb a walled track to East Stonesdale Farm, entering the farmyard through a metal gate.

■ **2** Now bear left, leaving the Pennine Way and staying with the Coast to Coast, along a finely surfaced farm track from where the views of Keld and the Swale below are beautiful. The track first contours the valley side, then descends to bridge Stonesdale Beck near a lovely waterfall and finally climbs to join a minor road on a bend.

■ **3** Cross it diagonally to a signposted gate, clearly seen, which you go through and continue along the top of a sloping field, close to a wall on your right, aiming for the top of Cotterby Scar. Take the easy-to-follow path westwards, close to a cliff top fence on your left, using ladder stiles and passing, below the cliff, beautiful Wain Wath Force.

■ **4** On reaching a rough farm track go up right, along it, passing Smithy Holme, a deserted farm. The track climbs steadily, sweeping right, and deteriorates to become a spongy green path as it approaches and passes the rim of Oven Mouth at the southern end of dramatic How Edge Scars, where, far below, the impressive Whitsundale Beck tumbles. Continue through gated fields along a clear path and at the northern end of the Scars, where the path bifurcates, go right, along the higher one, to a gate in a facing wall, waymarked with a yellow dot. Ravenseat is clearly seen ahead and the descent to it is gentle, well waymarked and easy to follow.

SECTION B	3.75 Miles (6 Km)		
Destination	Tan Hill Inn (GR 897067)		
Ascent	250m(821ft)	Descent	110m(361ft)

■ **5** On reaching the two-house hamlet continue in front of the farmhouse on your right and along a passage between an outbuilding on your right and the beck which you cross on a footbridge slightly upstream of a fine packhorse bridge. Almost at once turn right, through some sheep pens, and continue upstream to ford it immediately above Jenny Whalley Force.

■ **6** Having forded the beck, take the rising farm track ahead. Cross a clearly seen nearby stile into a huge pasture. Climb up it, edging a ghyll on your right, guided by post waymarkers. The climb is steep but the overall panoramic views are magnificent. Where the ghyll curves right, continue straight ahead aiming for a TV mast seen on the horizon. On reaching it follow a narrow trod right towards nearby ruinous Robert's Seat House on the 537m (1762ft) contour. The trod passes in front of the ruin, then immediately bears left and, soon after leaving it, reaches a stile in a facing fence.

■ **7** Cross the stile and go straight ahead along a narrow clear trod, descending gradually, following the rim of West Stones Dale to reach Tongue Sike after a mile of superb fell walking. Continue on the narrow trod to the left of the ghyll (another path to the right of the ghyll is often used by walkers but is not a P.R.O.W.). On approaching the more incised Thomas Gill, curve right and cross Tongue Sike, then descend towards a sheepfold and confluence of this beck and Stonesdale Beck.

■ **8** Keeping the stream to your left, cross the Stonesdale Beck and turn left upstream. (The route used by many walkers passes to the left of the sheepfold and bearing right to bridge the Stonesdale Beck, is not a P.R.O.W.). Immediately go left, upstream. Where the path fades simply stay close to the beckside. Soon after passing another sheepfold on the far bank cross a small feeder coming from the right and immediately skirt an outcrop to bend round right and continue along a thin, clear path close to and parallel to this feeder on your right.

■ **9** After crossing an area of coarse grasses the path makes a short, steep climb, edges a short ghyll and joins a minor road at a footpath sign. Turn left along this road for about 300 metres until you meet a road junction. Turn right to the Tan Hill Inn some 100 metres ahead.

SECTION C	4.25 Miles (6.8 Km)		
Destination	Keld (GR 893012)		
Ascent	14m(46ft)	Descent	210m(698ft)

■ **10** The Pennine Way is rejoined at Tan Hill. It is a broad track going south on slightly rising ground. After about ½ mile, when the track curves left at a footpath sign, leave it for a less obvious path, as directed, going right, passing some peat channels and within 150 metres of your route, two very dangerous abandoned mine shafts. It is advisable to stick to the known way.

■ **11** A mile south of Tan Hill bear right, descending a cairned route, along Lad Gill Hill and cross Lad Gill.

■ **12** From Lad Gill the moorland path can be very soggy but is clear and as High Frith Farm is approached the path becomes a stony track and remains easy to follow. Continue along it, contouring and keeping roughly parallel to Stonesdale Beck below on your right with, and beyond, the Keld to Tan Hill road, soon to pass below Frith Lodge on your left, leaving the track.

■ **13** Ahead, as Black Moor is crossed, there are good views ahead of Great Shunner Fell and Lovely Seat. On approaching Keld the route descends and enters a walled track which leads to East Stonesdale, from where you retrace your steps to Keld, so ending a splendid, good weather walk.

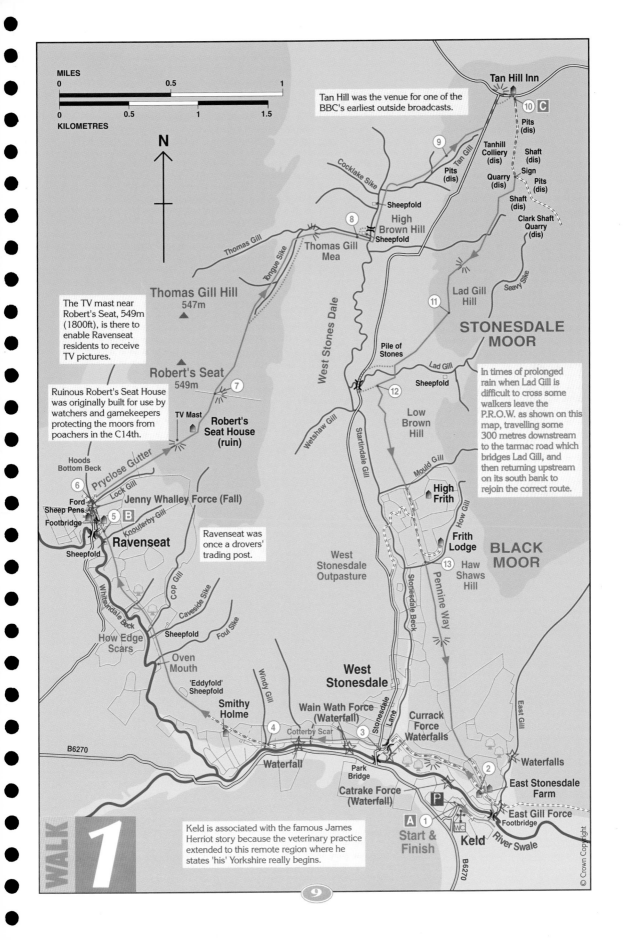

MILES

0   0.5   1

0   0.5   1   1.5

KILOMETRES

N

Tan Hill was the venue for one of the BBC's earliest outside broadcasts.

Tan Hill Inn

⑩ Ⓒ

Pits (dis)

Tanhill Colliery (dis)

Shaft (dis)

Sign

Quarry (dis)

Pits (dis)

Shaft (dis)

Clark Shaft Quarry (dis)

⑨

Tan Gill

Cocklake Sike

Pits (dis)

Pits (dis)

Sheepfold

⑧

High Brown Hill

Sheepfold

Thomas Gill

Thomas Gill Mea

Thomas Gill

Tongue Sike

Lad Gill Hill

Seavy Sike

The TV mast near Robert's Seat, 549m (1800ft), is there to enable Ravenseat residents to receive TV pictures.

Thomas Gill Hill
547m ▲

West Stones Dale

⑪

STONESDALE MOOR

Pile of Stones

Lad Gill

▲ **Robert's Seat**
549m   ⑦

Ruinous Robert's Seat House was originally built for use by watchers and gamekeepers protecting the moors from poachers in the C14th.

TV Mast

Robert's Seat House (ruin)

Pryclose Gutter

Hoods Bottom Beck

Lock Gill

⑥

Ford
Sheep Pens
Footbridge

⑤ Ⓑ

Ravenseat

Sheepfold

Knouterby Gill

Welshaw Gill

Startindale Gill

Sheepfold

⑫

Low Brown Hill

In times of prolonged rain when Lad Gill is difficult to cross some walkers leave the P.R.O.W. as shown on this map, travelling some 300 metres downstream to the tarmac road which bridges Lad Gill, and then returning upstream on its south bank to rejoin the correct route.

Jenny Whalley Force (Fall)

Ravenseat was once a drovers' trading post.

Cop Gill

Caveside Sike

Foul Sike

Whitsundale Beck

How Edge Scars

Sheepfold

Oven Mouth

'Eddyfold' Sheepfold

Smithy Holme

Windy Gill

High Frith

Frith Lodge

How Gill

BLACK MOOR

Haw Shaws Hill

⑬

Mould Gill

West Stonesdale Outpasture

Stonesdale Beck

Pennine Way

West Stonesdale

B6270

④

Cotterby Scar

Wain Wath Force (Waterfall)

③

Stonesdale Lane

Currack Force Waterfalls

East Gill

Waterfall

Waterfalls

②

East Stonesdale Farm

Park Bridge

Ⓟ

Catrake Force (Waterfall)

Ⓐ ①

Ⓜ

East Gill Force
Footbridge

Start & Finish

Keld

River Swale

B6270

Keld is associated with the famous James Herriot story because the veterinary practice extended to this remote region where he states 'his' Yorkshire really begins.

WALK

1

© Crown Copyright

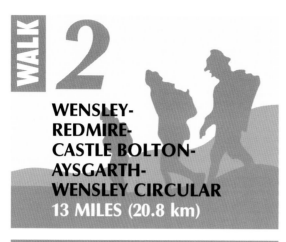

WALK 2

WENSLEY-REDMIRE-CASTLE BOLTON-AYSGARTH-WENSLEY CIRCULAR

13 MILES (20.8 km)

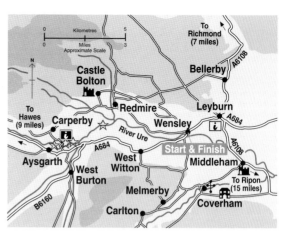

Route Details

Distance	13 miles (20.8 km)
Degree of Difficulty	Moderate
Ascent	131m (430ft)
Time	7 hours

Start and Finish Points

Wensley, now a delightful, sleepy village, lies close to the River Ure on the A684, a mile south-west of Leyburn. It marks the downstream end of upper Wensleydale, where the River Ure breaks free from the confines of the dale to follow a meandering course down the Vale of York. Mid-way through the village, stands the post box and this grand circular starts and finishes here.

Maps Needed

OS Outdoor Leisure No 30 (1:25 000)

Parking Facilities

There is limited roadside parking in Wensley, but please check with the local inhabitants first.

Short Cuts

On leaving Castle Bolton, where the route would take you through more pleasant field walking, and bring you to the River Ure, take the road downhill from the western end of the village, the castle end.

Continue in a south-easterly direction to a T-junction with the Carperby to Redmire road. Turn left, eastwards, along it, returning to Redmire to find yourself at the point where the road turns sharp left, rejoining the outward route at point (3), and retrace your steps to Wensley.

Route Summary

This spectacular circular makes a purposeful and most pleasing start through beautiful parkland. It fronts Bolton Hall, edges the Ure as a clear forest track and continues to Redmire over a succession of stiled fields. Mostly field walking lies between Redmire and Castle Bolton and this pleasing pattern is repeated all the way to the spectacular Aysgarth Falls.

The majestic Bolton Castle in the tiny village of Castle Bolton

On the return, from a clearly defined riverside path the falls can be admired from a different angle. Then the route leaves the river, but only briefly, and this delightful walk returns to the riverbank, to which it clings for most of the way back to Wensley. This allows you to visit another spectacular waterfall, Redmire Force.

Throughout, the riverside scenery is idyllic. For the most part this beautiful downstream section is through a succession of fields with a clear path edging riverside woodland for the final mile to the road bridge over the Ure just south of Wensley. Cross the bridge and before you know it you will be back at the start, wondering how such a pleasant walk had reached its end so quickly.

Interesting Features

GEOLOGY Valley soils come mainly from glacial deposits, clays, gravels and sands. Anglican settlers favoured morainic gravels and frequently sited their settlements on them, the 'ley' endings of their place names reflecting these good, gravelly soils. Wensley is an Anglican settlement and Wensleydale is named after it, not from a river as are most of the other dales.

Repeated layers of limestone, shale and sandstone dating from Carboniferous times, some 300 million years ago and named as the Yoredale series by geologist Philips are at their most exposed in Yoredale, the old name for Wensleydale, and provide some of the dale's finest scenery.

LANDFORMS Aysgarth is renowned for its falls - Upper, Middle and Lower - which are terrifying when the River Ure is in spate. Yore Bridge, just below the Upper Falls was first built as a nine-foot-wide packhorse bridge in 1594.

The famous triple falls at Aysgarth bring a touch of the picturesque.

HISTORY Until 1563, when it was struck by plague, Wensley had been the market town of the dale for more than 200 years. This disaster is noted in the parish register of crops for that year with these gloomy words: 'This year nothing set down'.

Wensley's Holy Trinity church, probably the finest in the dale, was built in 1245 on Saxon foundations. The wall paintings in the nave are thought to date from about 1330 and are among the oldest in Yorkshire. The church also contains old pews, once used by the Bolton family of Castle Bolton, a 14th century memorial brass and some 16th century choir stalls.

The Boltons built Bolton Hall in 1678 because Castle Bolton, their old home, had become uninhabitable following serious neglect during the Civil War. It was a wise move as later events proved. In 1761 the north-east tower of the castle suddenly collapsed.

Redmire is a pleasant surprise, a cluster of charming dwellings, some set about a green, a village pump, an ancient tree with creaking limbs resting on wooden crutches, two pubs, and a pillar with a tale to tell. It was erected when the village was supplied with lamps to mark Queen Victoria's Golden Jubilee and electric light was fitted to it to commemorate the Silver Jubilee of Elizabeth II.

Bolton Castle, whose massive bulk is visible from so many points along the valley, was once the home of the Scropes, one of the most powerful families in mediaeval England. Probably of Norman extraction, the Scropes had arrived in Wensley by 1205. By 1285 they owned land at East Bolton, as Castle Bolton was then called.

The natural splendour of Aysgarth Lower Falls

In 1568, following her defeat at Longside, Mary, Queen of Scots, was held at Castle Bolton for six months. During that time, with the help of a local man, Kit Norton of Rylstone, she gave the guards the slip one night, only to be caught at a place now known as Queen's Gap, on Leyburn Shawl, a long natural terrace that runs parallel to the valley. Her freedom had lasted two hours.

Between the bridge and beautifully sited Aysgarth Church there is an old corn mill that was originally a cotton mill and later became a worsted mill, spinning yarn for the hand knitters of the dale. The sudden development of machinery left it with six hundred dozen jerseys unsold. These were eventually dyed red and sent to Italy where they became the red coats of Garibaldi's Army of Unification. In 1853 the mill was burned down and rebuilt the same year. In the early 19th century one room was used as a school. Today it is a carriage museum.

PEOPLE Surgeon Beatty, who attended fatally wounded Lord Nelson on HMS Victory at the Battle of Trafalgar on 21st October, 1805, is buried in Wensley churchyard.

Cross-Section of the Route

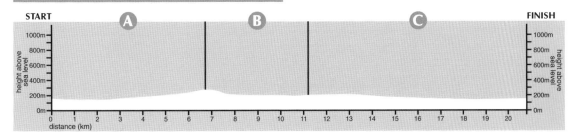

Route Description

SECTION A	4.25 Miles (6.8 Km)		
Destination	Castle Bolton (GR 036919)		
Ascent	120m(394ft)	Descent	3m(9ft)

■ 1 From Wensley's post box cross the road and go through the entrance to Bolton Hall. Follow the concrete road through the Hall grounds, passing Middle Lodge, some tall beeches, a larch plantation and Bolton Hall on your right. When you reach a crossing of tracks continue ahead on a muddy farm track, first edging the left side of a plantation, then cutting through it on rising ground, with the River Ure below you on your left.

■ 2 On reaching the edge of the wood, where the track splits, go left briefly and exit through the kissing gate, clearly seen ahead. Follow a clear path, cross five stiled fields and in the sixth one keep close to the hedge on your right. Exit through a right-hand corner stile into an enclosed farm track. Continue, right, along it, to join surfaced Wood End Lane and turn left, along it, to Redmire.

■ 3 At a junction turn right and go up the village, then left, opposite the village pump. Continue ahead, passing an ancient tree and the village green on your right, go directly over cross-roads and past the Bolton Arms on your left. Continue along the road to cross a waymarked stile on your left.

■ 4 Follow the path edging a house, cross a stile and a small pasture to reach Apedale Beck which is crossed by striding from stone to stone, there being no bridge. Once across it go through a stile immediately to the right of a wall which is approached end on. Cross the next two fields to a facing stile, go diagonally right over the next one to a stile onto a disused railway. Go diagonally left to cross another stile. Turn left, bridge a beck and go diagonally right, up the next field, to a stile. Bear left across the next field to a stile to the left of a dutch barn. Cross the next field to a stile in a facing wall, beyond which go right, along a track into Castle Bolton village where you turn left to join the road.

SECTION B	2.75 Miles (4.4 Km)		
Destination	Yore Bridge (GR 011886)		
Ascent	0m(0ft)	Descent	52m(161ft)

■ 5 On reaching the castle turn left, along the road, and on reaching a signposted bridleway turn right, along the track. Continue beyond the last house to the disused line. Cross a stile and turn right to climb another stile. Cross the next field diagonally left to a gate in a hedge near some trees at the end of a section of wall. Keeping in the same direction go diagonally across the corner of the next field to a facing gate. Cross the next field and exit at a stile at its bottom right-hand corner onto a road at a bend.

■ 6 Go right, along it, over the bridge and when the road curves right go through a second gate on your left and along a farm track. Where it bends left, go right and exit through a stile in a wall on your right. Go diagonally left over the next field, leaving it through a gate onto a track. Take this track towards a dutch barn, then left, then right towards High Thoresby, seen ahead.

■ 7 On approaching the farm fork left, past the right side of a barn marked with a yellow dot, into a field where you go right to exit through a facing gate onto a farm track between ruined outbuildings.

■ 8 On entering a field, go diagonally right, exiting at a stile in the field corner. Immediately cross another stile to the right and keep in the same direction on rising ground to a soon-to-be-seen signposted stile, which you climb over. Go left along a farm track to Hollins House Farm.

■ 9 Where the track splits go left, past the side of the farmhouse, guided by markers. Go through a gate into a field and follow a clear track through a gate and down a field. Where the track curves left, continue ahead to cross a stile, continue close to a fence on your right and go left at a 'Footpath to Castle Bolton' sign. Descend to join a riverside path and follow it upstream, passing Aysgarth's Lower and Middle Falls which can be viewed in complete safety. When the path reaches a road turn left, along it, to cross Yore Bridge just below High Falls.

SECTION C	6 Miles (9.6Km)		
Destination	Wensley (GR 092896)		
Ascent	11m(36ft)	Descent	76m(235ft)

■ 10 Immediately over Yore Bridge climb steps to St Andrew's Church, going round the front of it and down a fenced path between tombstones to a stile. Climb this field, diagonally right, to a stile into a shallow wood. Go through it on a clear path, exiting at a stile. Cross the fields ahead, as signposted, passing the falls on your left. This clear path soon descends alongside the river to a signpost. Go diagonally right, as indicated, across a field to the road. Go left, along it, over Hestholme Beck, beyond where you go left over a signposted stile.

■ 11 Pass to the left of a field house, following arrows, and bear right, through a gate. Continue to another gate and pass the front of Adam Bottoms Farm. Cross its exit road and bear left to a facing ladder-stile, following painted arrows. Continue down the riverbank and climb a wooded bank on entering it. On leaving it on the bank top go diagonally left, up the field to a sign at a wire fence on your right, which you follow to cross a stile. Immediately cross another stile on your left and continue along a bank top to another stile, cutting off a curve in the River Ure.

■ 12 Keep along this higher ground, close to a wall on your left, edging a wood and crossing facing stiles. On going through a gate into a wood go left, down steps to spectacular Redmire Force, climbing from it along a clear path to leave the wood through another gate. Cross the field ahead along a depression, using a faint green track to a ladder-stile.

■ 13 The way ahead is waymarked and stiled and is never far away from the river. On reaching Wensley Bridge cross it and continue up the road to Wensley.

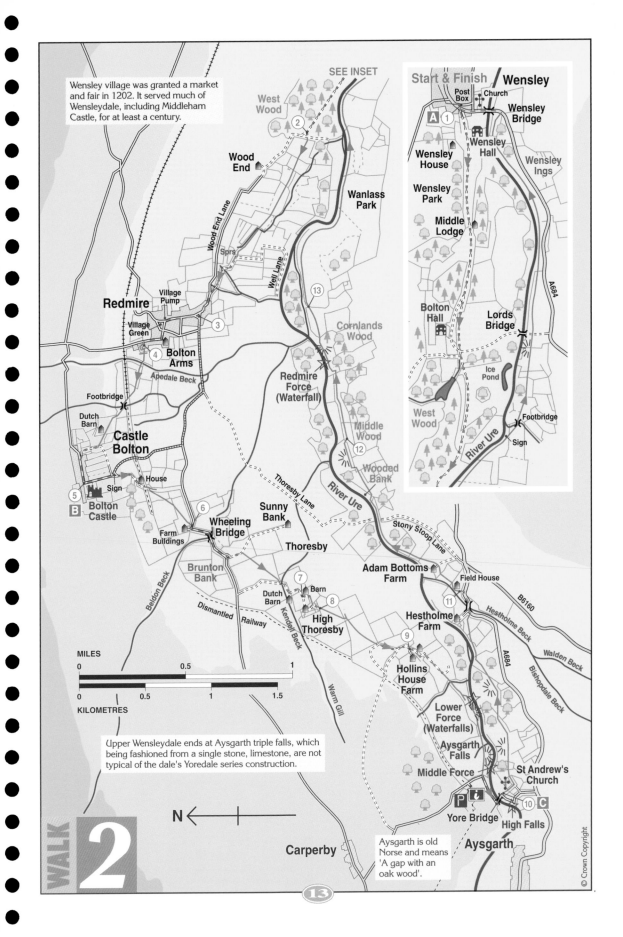

Wensley village was granted a market and fair in 1202. It served much of Wensleydale, including Middleham Castle, for at least a century.

SEE INSET

West Wood

Wood End

Wanlass Park

Start & Finish   **Wensley**

Post Box
Church
Wensley Bridge
A 1
Wensley Hall
Wensley House
Wensley Ings
Wensley Park
Middle Lodge
Bolton Hall
Lords Bridge
Ice Pond
West Wood
River Ure
Footbridge
Sign
A684

Wood End Lane

Sprs

Well Lane

13

Cornlands Wood

Redmire

Village Pump

Village Green

3

4

Bolton Arms

Apedale Beck

Redmire Force (Waterfall)

Middle Wood

12

Footbridge

Dutch Barn

Castle Bolton

Wooded Bank

River Ure

Thoresby Lane

5 Sign House
B
Bolton Castle

Farm Buildings

6

Wheeling Bridge

Sunny Bank

Stony Stoop Lane

Thoresby

Adam Bottoms Farm

Field House

11

B6160

Hestholme Beck

Brunton Bank

Beldon Beck

Dismantled Railway

Dutch Barn

7

Barn

8

High Thoresby

Kendell Beck

Hestholme Farm

Walden Beck

9

Hollins House Farm

A684

Bishopdale Beck

MILES
0   0.5   1

0   0.5   1   1.5
KILOMETRES

Warm Gill

Lower Force (Waterfalls)

Aysgarth Falls

Middle Force

St Andrew's Church

Upper Wensleydale ends at Aysgarth triple falls, which being fashioned from a single stone, limestone, are not typical of the dale's Yoredale series construction.

N ←———|———

P

10 **C**

Yore Bridge

High Falls

Carperby

Aysgarth is old Norse and means 'A gap with an oak wood'.

Aysgarth

© Crown Copyright

WALK **2**

13

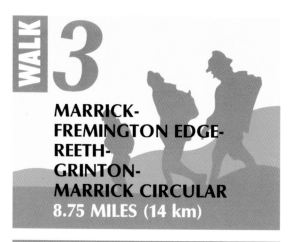

WALK 3

MARRICK-FREMINGTON EDGE-REETH-GRINTON-MARRICK CIRCULAR

8.75 MILES (14 km)

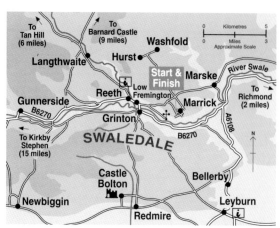

Route Details

Distance	8.75 miles (14 km)
Degree of Difficulty	Moderate
Ascent	252m (827ft)
Time	5 hours

Start and Finish Points

Marrick is an airy hamlet perched high above the north bank of the River Swale, a good two miles downstream of Reeth. It is best reached by taking a minor road eastwards from the eastern end of Low Fremington for one and a half miles, then turning right at a junction for about a mile. This walk starts and finishes in the north-west corner of Marrick at a small, triangular green/junction with a viewing seat.

Maps Needed

OS Outdoor Leisure No 30 (1:25 000)
OS Landranger No 98 (1:50 000)
OS Landranger No 99 (1:50 000)

Parking Facilities

There is limited roadside parking in Marrick, but please check with the locals first.

Short Cuts

Should deteriorating weather conditions catch you unawares during the walk's early stages, on reaching the minor road at New Close Bank, turn left, along it, descending to Low Fremington from where the route can be rejoined at Reeth Bridge and completed well below cloud level.

If, on reaching the Marrick Priory Road, you feel jiggered, instead of crossing it to point (14), turn right, along it, to rejoin the route at point (16).

Route Summary

The first section of this gloriously varied circular is high level, over rough pastures, beyond which a short road walk leads onto Fremington Edge and borders Marrick Moor, which is seen at its magnificent best in the autumn when blooming heather transforms it into a sea of purple.

A steep and exhilarating descent brings you close to Arkle Beck, which is followed for a while before being crossed on Reeth Bridge.

There are hotels, pubs and cafes in Reeth, the apex of the walk, making it an ideal place for a 'butty' stop.

A splendid view from Reeth village green to Fremington Edge

From Reeth the easy-to-follow route descends to cross the River Swale on a swing bridge and continues downstream, never far from the soothing sound of flowing waters, to Grinton with its splendid church. Here the Swale is re-crossed and more glorious riverside walking follows.

The approach to ruinous Marrick Priory is across lush green fields; and from it a steep climb up a wooded scarp, using a stepped path, will bring you safely back to the quiet hamlet of Marrick replete with contentment.

Interesting Features

GEOLOGY Like many dales villages and hamlets, Marrick is cleverly situated on well drained soil high above the valley flood plain on a limestone terrace, showing that early settlers knew a good site when they saw one. It shares the 300 metres (1,000ft) contour with Keld at the head of Swaledale and Whaw in Arkengarthdale.

LANDFORMS A viewpoint is shown on the map where the Marske road reaches Reels Head, slightly west of where the route turns right. By making a short detour to it you will be rewarded with excellent views. Viewpoints unfold throughout the walk and their unexpectedness adds to the walks charm.

Compare Norse Upper Swaledale, seen to advantage from Fremington Edge, with neighbouring Anglo-Saxon Wensleydale, seen to advantage from Leyburn Shawl, and at once great differences become evident. In Wensleydale the settlements are evenly spread along both sides of the valley, through which two roads thread: in Swaledale with only one road running along it, the settlements are sited on only one side of the valley, the one receiving most sun.

HISTORY The Anglo-Saxon settlement of the dales, well established by the middle of the 7th century, did not extend further up Swaledale than Reeth because the valley was too narrow and wild to suit Anglian farming. By the mid-9th century Danish raiders had infiltrated Swaledale as far as Reeth, sometimes taking over and renaming Anglian villages. Not until the 10th century was Upper Swaledale colonised; and this time the settlers were Norse, the descendants of those Norsemen who had settled along the eastern side of Ireland. They came from the west, along the Eden Valley, by Stainmore and Mallerstang and built their homesteads mainly on the south facing side of the valley.

Marrick Priory was founded as a nunnery by Roger-de-Aske during the reign of King Stephen 'when Christ and his saint slept'. Today it is an Outward Bound Centre. Archery is practiced just inside the Priory grounds; and judging by the nearby rows of headstones a lot more practice is needed!

Disused mine shafts to the west of Marrick belong to the history of lead mining in Swaledale and some distance away from them are the remains of two smelting mills.

The site is a complex one. A double flue joins the two mills and the lower one is the older of the two. The present remains are 19th century but they stand on the site of a 16th century building.

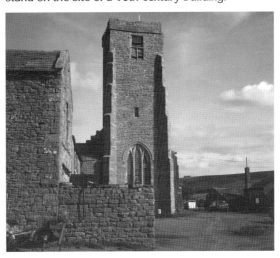

The ancient remains of Marrick Priory

The higher mill was built between 1747 and 1778 when the mines together with the lower smelting mill were leased to the London (Quaker) Lead Company. At that time the lower mill had a chimney, up which the fumes from the ore heaths were extracted. When the lower mill was rebuilt, a double flue was built up the hill to the base of the chimney of the higher mill; and along it the fumes from the lower hearths were drawn to escape out of the chimney of the higher mill. At this time the higher mill was out of use because the flue from the lower mill passed under the ore hearth of the higher mill. When, around the middle of the 19th century, the higher mill was reconstructed the flues from the lower mill were blocked off. From then on the lower mill was not used because there was no exit for the fumes. At that time the wheel pit in the Upper Building was extended and since the pit of the higher mill was comparable in size with that of the bottom mill, the wheel may have been transferred from the lower mill to the higher mill. This mill closed circa 1890. The remains of Marrick Smelting Mills are perhaps the most important of earlier small scale lead smelting to be found in Britain.

Cross-Section of the Route

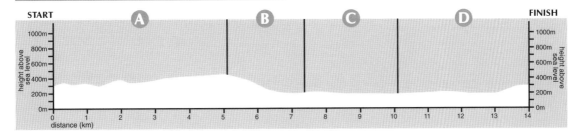

Route Description

SECTION A — 3 Miles (4.8 Km)

Destination	Fremington Edge Top (GR 044006)
Ascent 114m(374ft)	Descent 26m(85ft)

■ **1** From the small, triangular junction at the north-west corner of Marrick take the quiet road, north-westwards, passing a farm on your left and continue to cross a rise. On descending the other side of it go left, over a stile in a wall which is marked with a footpath sign.

■ **2** Cross the field ahead, close to a wall on your right and as you climb a hillside towards an enclosure go through a wall gap marked with a yellow dot on your right. Immediately turn left and continue close to the wall, now on your left, to a gate in a facing wall. Reeth, with its fine Calver backcloth, and a superb view of Upper Swaledale are seen directly ahead. Continue straight ahead, still with the wall on your left to reach a signposted metal gate, which you go through onto a road.

■ **3** Turn right, along it, and where it bends right at a 'Marrick: 1 mile' signpost go through a stile in the wall on your left and follow the faint track to a facing gate, which you go through. Continue along this track, close to a wall on your left, climbing steadily, and continue to reach a heather moor. The track is very broad indeed and it edges Fremington Edge.

■ **4** When a cairn is passed and the track peters out continue ahead. Cross a facing wall on a ladder-stile with an old disused radio mast over the wall on the left. Continue over marshland to cross a wooden fence, using a stile waymarked with yellow dots.

SECTION B — 1.25 Miles (2 Km)

Destination	Reeth (GR 038993)
Ascent 19m(62ft)	Descent 234m(768ft)

■ **5** Over this stile, go left, through a gate in the wall and, follow the clear track down the escarpment. From here, the whole of Reeth is spread out: it is a wonderful sight.

■ **6** Descend towards a footpath sign, prominent above a white cottage, going through a gate and still on the track. Turn sharp right on reaching the sign and continue descending, now diagonally right to a black, wooden gate in a wall, which you go through.

■ **7** Continue diagonally left, downhill, crossing a very uneven pasture along a faint, meandering path. At the bottom, cross a stile in a facing wall to the right of a gate. Cross the next field, going to the right of a field house with a white arrow on it, aiming for a stile in a facing wall, which you go through.

■ **8** Cross the next small field and continue along the top of a tree-lined bank, on a clear path approaching Arkle Beck. Leave the field through a waymarked stile at the left-hand side of a facing wall. Continue, bearing right and aiming for the road bridge over Arkle Beck. Go through the left of two facing gates. Cross the next field to the signposted stile onto the road and go right over Arkle Beck.

■ **9** Immediately turn left and double back along a signposted footpath and go under the bridge to a stile and follow a path upstream. When a footpath sign that points left, is reached, go left, through the gate, leaving the beckside path.

■ **10** Cross a small field and climb a steep and narrow walled path. Once past some dwellings, you emerge onto a cobbled lane. Turn right, uphill, onto the village green in Reeth.

SECTION C — 1.75 Miles (2.8 Km)

Destination	Grinton (GR 046984)
Ascent 0m(0ft)	Descent 18m(59ft)

■ **11** Bear left, across the green to its south-west corner. Leave between houses along a pathway signposted 'To the River', which enters a lane before reaching a road junction. Turn left to the road end, then right, along a lane, passing the doctor's surgery. At the end of this lane turn left, down a walled path and go through a gate. Bear right at the fence corner to cross a small footbridge and continue to cross the Swale on a swing bridge.

■ **12** Turn left, aiming for a stile next to a gate on your left and cross two fields, downstream. At the field corner go through two gates into a walled path and follow it to reach a lane. Turn left, along it, towards Grinton. On reaching Grinton churchyard turn left down steps, and follow a riverside path to enter Grinton between the church and the vicarage.

SECTION D — 2.75 Miles (4.4 Km)

Destination	Marrick (GR 075982)
Ascent 119m(391ft)	Descent 8m(26ft)

■ **13** Turn left, passing The Bridge Inn on your right, bridge the Swale and immediately turn sharp right along a waymarked riverside path to reach a surfaced road. Turn left, uphill, soon to turn right over a stile opposite a metal gate and enter a field.

■ **14** Contour this steep field, bearing slightly left with rising ground to reach a stile in a facing fence. Cross this small enclosure to a stile in a facing wall. Now follow the indistinct path in a south-easterly direction, contouring across stiled and gated fields.

■ **15** Keep ahead across a field with a field house in the far left-hand corner. Continue across the stiled and gated fields, bearing slightly right and ignoring any paths leading to Ince Wood. Keep bearing right, aiming for the tower of Marrick Priory. Go to the right of a gate in a fenced field corner and descend the grassy path towards farm buildings and go through a gate.

■ **16** Turn left along a surfaced lane, passing the farm and Marrick Priory.

■ **17** Just past the entrance to the Priory bear left through a waymarked gate. Ascend along a clear path into a wooded scar and continue up it, using a stepped path.

■ **18** On leaving the wood, edge the field ahead close to a wall on your right. Go through two gates and continue to reach an enclosed lane back into Marrick where it all began.

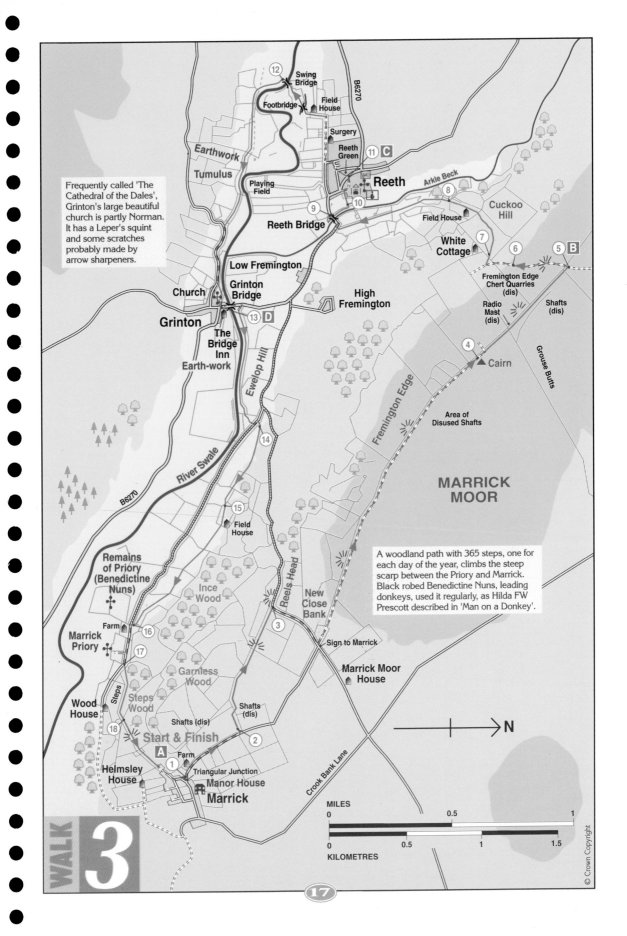

Frequently called 'The Cathedral of the Dales', Grinton's large beautiful church is partly Norman. It has a Leper's squint and some scratches probably made by arrow sharpeners.

A woodland path with 365 steps, one for each day of the year, climbs the steep scarp between the Priory and Marrick. Black robed Benedictine Nuns, leading donkeys, used it regularly, as Hilda FW Prescott described in 'Man on a Donkey'.

Swing Bridge
Footbridge
Field House
Surgery
Reeth Green
Reeth
Arkle Beck
Cuckoo Hill
Field House
White Cottage
Fremington Edge Chert Quarries (dis)
Radio Mast (dis)
Shafts (dis)
Earthwork
Tumulus
Playing Field
Reeth Bridge
Low Fremington
Grinton Bridge
Church
Grinton
High Fremington
The Bridge Inn
Earth-work
Ewelop Hill
Fremington Edge
Cairn
Grouse Butts
MARRICK MOOR
Area of Disused Shafts
River Swale
Reels Head
New Close Bank
Remains of Priory (Benedictine Nuns)
Ince Wood
Field House
Farm
Marrick Priory
Garnless Wood
Marrick Moor House
Sign to Marrick
Wood House
Steps
Steps Wood
Shafts (dis)
Shafts (dis)
Start & Finish
Farm
Helmsley House
Triangular Junction
Manor House
Marrick
Crook Bank Lane

B6270

N

MILES
0   0.5   1

KILOMETRES
0   0.5   1   1.5

WALK 3

17

© Crown Copyright

HORSEHOUSE-
SWINESIDE-
HINDLETHWAITE-
ARKLESIDE MOOR-
HORSEHOUSE CIRCULAR
7.5 MILES (12 km)

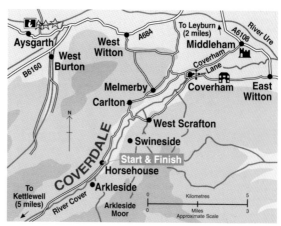

Route Details

Distance	7.5 miles (12 km)
Degree of Difficulty	Moderate
Ascent	241m (790ft)
Time	4.5 hours

Start and Finish Points

The hamlet of Horsehouse lies deep in Coverdale and is best reached by taking a minor road, Coverham Lane, south-westwards from Middleham via Carlton.

The only approach from the west is along the same steep road from its other end, at Kettlewell. This exhilarating circular begins outside the Thwaite Arms, Horsehouse, and if your timing is right, ends inside it!

Maps Needed

OS Outdoor Leisure No 30 (1:25 000)

Parking Facilities

There is limited roadside parking in Horsehouse, but please check with the local residents first.

Short Cuts

If tired or in deteriorating visibility or weather conditions, a quick descent from the high ground can be achieved by turning right instead of left immediately after Arkleside Gill has been crossed at point (9). This clear and straight track descends quickly to rejoin the route at point (15) where it skirts left of Arkleside Farm. The track is then re-joined and goes to the valley road, reaching it about half a mile west of Horsehouse.

Route Summary

From the valley bottom the walk crosses the River Cover and almost at once the long, slanting climb to Swineside Farm begins. The ascent is quite steep and several becks are crossed before the route begins to level out and contour across fields.

From Swineside Farm the southwards crossing of first Swineside Moor, then Hindlethwaite Moor presents little difficulty.

Once Arkleside Gill is passed and a clear track is reached it is simply a matter of staying on it as it climbs to reach a National Park boundary fence in a dip between Little Whernside and Dead Man's Hill.

The pretty expanses of Coverdale near Horsehouse

Here the descent to the valley bottom begins. Undefined in parts, it keeps close to the left edge of Harkera Gill. It is here that Harkera Gill is crossed, beyond which there follows a delightful level section through fields, running parallel to the River Cover. The course of the walk is direct and leads below Arkleside Farm onto a farm road.

The road keeps alongside the river, then crosses it to join the road that threads the valley bottom. Within half a mile the hamlet of Horsehouse is reached and the walk is completed.

Interesting Features

GEOLOGY Today, farming predominates in Coverdale where once quarrying for sandstone flags was an important industry. The valley, lying between Wharfedale and Wensleydale is right in the heart of the true Yoredale country. Here the Great Scar limestone of the southern dales has dipped in height and the limestone layers are thinner, but the pattern remains constant; a sandwich of limestone, then shale, then sandstone, repeated again and again with only the thicknesses varying.

LANDFORMS The hogback of West Scrafton Moor, Dead Man's Hill and Little Whernside with the hollows between them, give the southern side of Coverdale a convoluted look. The moors of East and West Scrafton, Swineside, Hindlethwaite and Arkleside provide some of the finest grouse shooting in Yorkshire.

The River Cover rises near Great and Little Whernside on the North Moor above Starbotton in Wharfedale and waters Coverdale, making it fertile.

In Horsehouse churchyard, there stands an ample weeping beech, a graceful mass of drooping, pendulous branches. It is well sited and attractive.

But the real charm of Coverdale lies not in this weeping beech; but in the natural beauty and grandeur of the whole valley of which this tree is a part, and the surrounding moors with their ever changing moods. The scenery is often spectacular, always interesting and never timid. This is further enhanced by the dramatic tonal sky effects which are constantly changing. This is what attracts landscape painters to Coverdale and this is what also attracts discerning walkers.

HISTORY Coverdale is to some extent a hidden, self-contained dale and has been so for more than 200 years. One road runs along the narrow valley bottom from Carlton over Park Rash, with its one in five gradients, to Kettlewell in Wharfedale. Quiet enough today to be incorporated into the Yorkshire Dales Cycle Way, it was once a busy highway. Soldiers marched along it to fight the Scots. Panoplied knights and their ladies, brilliantly arrayed nobles, historical giants who shaped the history of England, all made their stately way along Coverdale to and from Middleham Castle, the Windsor of the North, where, during the Wars of the Roses, Edward IV was held prisoner.

The Yorkshire Dales Railway opened in 1902, had been planned to continue up Wharfedale to Kettlewell from where it would continue under Great Whernside into Coverdale by means of a tunnel 3 miles long. It was then to run down the dale and swing into Wensleydale to join the N.E.R. between Leyburn and Hawes. The cost would have been prohibitive but what really enraged country lovers, who were supported by both John Ruskin and William Morris, was the proposed iron bridge across Aysgarth Falls. The opposition was formidable, the idea for the line was withdrawn and the Yorkshire Dales Railway terminated at Grassington.

The farming landscape surrounding Horsehouse in Coverdale

PEOPLE An itinerant called John Wilkinson, known as 'Scoury Stone Johnny', lived in Coverdale. He collected soft sandstone from Roova Crags which he sold for one old penny a piece on his rounds in the dales. He died in the 1920s.

A son of Coverdale, Miles Coverdale, 1488-1568, added lustre to the dale whose name he shared. He was a medieval scholar who translated the Scriptures. His version was known as 'The Great Bible'.

Carlton, the metropolis of the dale, is where Henry Constantine, the Coverdale bard, lived. A stone tablet dated 14th February 1861, commemorates him piously.

Isaac Cape of Tupgill, in Coverdale, became Lower Wensleydale's first professional horse trainer. He was appointed circa 1765.

Cross-Section of the Route

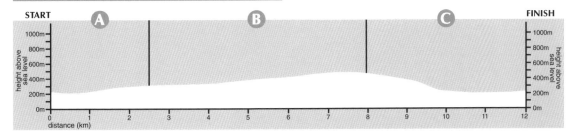

Route Description

SECTION A	1.5 Miles (2.4 Km)		
Destination	Bridleway, Swineside (GR 064824)		
Ascent	70m(230ft)	Descent	5m(16ft)

■ **1** From the Thwaite Arms, facing the road, go right and right again, down the side of the pub. Turn left along a lane, passing cottage gardens on your left. Turn right at an open space on your right, descending to a signposted gate. Continue diagonally left across two fields, as indicated, going to the right of a field house and through the right-hand of two gates in a facing wall. Keep ahead, cutting across the corner of the next field to cross the River Cover on a footbridge.

■ **2** Go forward, briefly, towards Hindlethwaite Hall, just ahead, then bear to the left of it and go through a gate in a wall on your left. Ignoring the farm track, go diagonally right across the field, climbing to a stile near the field corner, which you cross. Go slightly more to your right, aiming for the right-hand end of a wall, passing close to it and continuing in the same direction to cross Sealrigg Gill. Keep in roughly the same direction, climbing steadily to go through a facing stile at a point where the beck flows under it en route to Woods Gill.

■ **3** Now go diagonally right to a stile a quarter of the way along the wall on your right. Holding the same course, climb diagonally left to cross a stile two thirds of the way up another facing wall. Now contour the valley side, across Rampshaw Bank, to a stile in a facing wall. Still contouring, cross the next field parallel to a wall lower down on your left, leaving through a wall stile. Continue ahead, using stiles, towards Swineside Farm, now seen just ahead, reaching it over a stile and passing in front of the farmhouse to a tarmac road which links the farm and the hotel next door to West Scrafton.

■ **4** Turn right, along the road, climbing, and where it turns left, go right as indicated by a signpost, along a bridleway.

SECTION B	3 Miles (4.8 Km)		
Destination	NP Boundary Fence (GR 044783)		
Ascent	171m(561ft)	Descent	0m(0ft)

■ **5** The route is indistinct at times but the mean bearing is SSW across marshland, contouring close to the western edge of Swineside Moor, parallel to Middle Rigg, spread like a hogback to your left.

■ **6** After about ³/₄ mile the way, edged hereabouts with rushes, bears slightly left and goes through the remains of an old fence before going across Swineside Bogs, now an easy to follow path.

■ **7** Clearly seen ahead is Hindlethwaite Plantation. The route, very clear here, edges the top of the plantation, descending steeply to cross the beck above a waterfall and climbing up the gill's far side, where the way once more becomes indistinct. Continue southwards, on rising ground, climbing away from the wall on your right. Continue to go

through a gate in a facing fence and continue directly across the next two rough pastures.

■ **8** In the third one, on reaching Arkleside Gill slightly down stream of and parallel to a fence on your left, cross it and climb the far bank to a stile at the top. Should the beck be in spate go upstream to where the fence reaches it and make an easier crossing there. Having crossed at the fence, climb the far bank and go right, along its rim to cross the clearly seen stile onto a clear track.

■ **9** Turn left, along it, ascending steadily, and where it bifurcates take the right-hand fork with Pike Slack Gill on your left and, soon, a broken fence then a wall on your right. Soon after this wall ends the ground begins to level out. Continue, still on this clear track for a further ¹/₂ mile to reach the National Park boundary fence, the apex of the walk, mid-way between Dead Man's Hill and Little Whernside.

SECTION C	3 Miles (4.8 Km)		
Destination	Horsehouse (GR 047813)		
Ascent	4m(13ft)	Descent	241m(791ft)

■ **10** Turn right, crossing marshy Harkera Gill at its source and a stile in a fence, beyond which bear northwards, keeping the fence and the beck on your right using a bearing of 360 degrees north. Do not recross the gill because it very quickly develops into a formidable water course, tumbling down the steep and dramatic Harkera Gill. Eventually, as height is lost, the path becomes very clear.

■ **11** After about a mile of descent, where a second stream crosses your line of walk, scramble into and out of the shallow ravine containing it, the footbridge having collapsed. Continue descending to go through a gate in a facing wall close to the rim of Harkera Gill. Cross the field ahead to another stile over a fence on your right near the corner with a facing wall. Descend to cross Harkera Gill.

■ **12** Climb steps on the far side, cross a stile, cut the corner, left, to another stile and enter a field. Skirt the right side of this field to the building at the far right corner. Exit, right, at the corner into a long narrow enclosure and follow the farm track bearing left to the north-east. Keep the field boundary to your left and continue straight ahead to go through a gate, reaching the track to New Lathe on the left.

■ **13** Continuing in the same direction from this junction, pass a field on your left before the fenced track curves right.

■ **14** Bear left keeping to this track. Continue straight ahead passing two fields until you reach a gateway and a junction with a track coming in from the right.

■ **15** Enter the field on your left through a gated stile. Follow the route right, keeping Arkleside Farm on your right and skirting left of the enclosed field beyond it to rejoin the farm track at a footpath sign.

■ **16** Turn left, along it, first edging, then crossing the river at Arkleside Bridge to join the quiet minor road that threads the valley.

■ **17** Turn right along it for almost ¹/₂ mile back to Horsehouse.

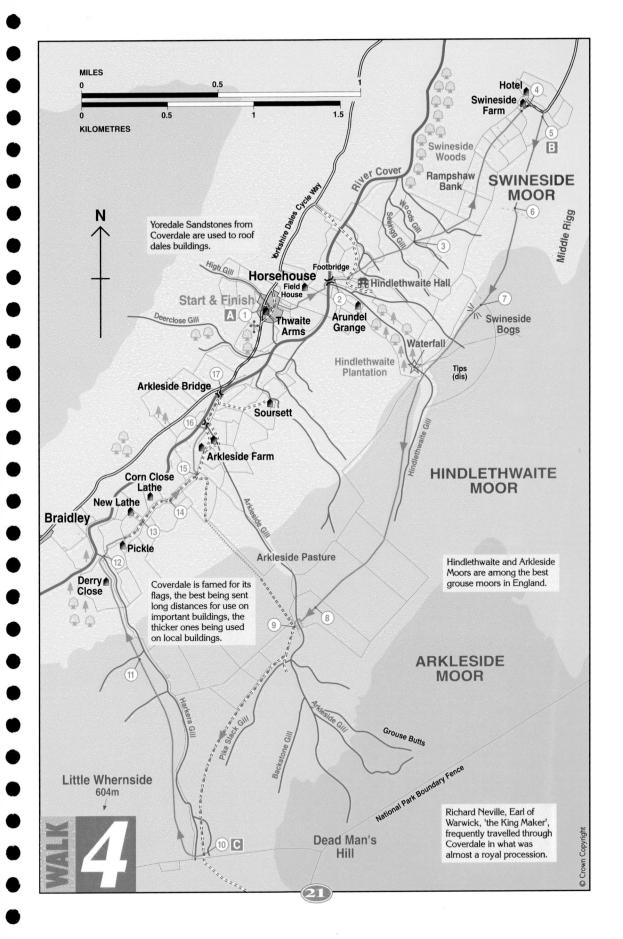

MILES
0   0.5   1

KILOMETRES
0   0.5   1   1.5

N

Yoredale Sandstones from
Coverdale are used to roof
dales buildings.

Yorkshire Dales Cycle Way

River Cover

Hotel
Swineside
Farm
④
⑤
Ⓑ

Swineside
Woods

Rampshaw
Bank

SWINESIDE
MOOR

Woods Gill

Seakeg Gill

③

⑥

Middle Rigg

High Gill

Horsehouse

Footbridge

Hindlethwaite Hall

Deerclose Gill

Start & Finish
Ⓐ ①

Field
House

Thwaite
Arms

②

Arundel
Grange

Waterfall

⑦

Swineside
Bogs

Hindlethwaite
Plantation

Tips
(dis)

Hindlethwaite Gill

⑰

Arkleside Bridge

⑯

Soursett

Arkleside Farm

Corn Close
Lathe

⑮

New Lathe

⑭

Braidley

⑬

Pickle

Arkleside Gill

Arkleside Pasture

HINDLETHWAITE
MOOR

Hindlethwaite and Arkleside
Moors are among the best
grouse moors in England.

⑫

Derry
Close

Coverdale is famed for its
flags, the best being sent
long distances for use on
important buildings, the
thicker ones being used
on local buildings.

⑨

⑧

ARKLESIDE
MOOR

⑪

Harkera Gill

Pike Slack Gill

Backstone Gill

Arkleside Gill

Grouse Butts

National Park Boundary Fence

Little Whernside
604m

WALK
4

⑩ Ⓒ

Dead Man's
Hill

Richard Neville, Earl of
Warwick, 'the King Maker',
frequently travelled through
Coverdale in what was
almost a royal procession.

© Crown Copyright

㉑

5

MIDDLEHAM-BRAITHWAITE HALL-COVERHAM-EAST WITTON-MIDDLEHAM CIRCULAR

8 MILES (12.8 km)

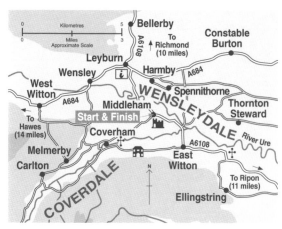

Route Details

Distance	8 miles (12.8 km)
Degree of Difficulty	Easy
Ascent	194m (636ft)
Time	5 hours

Start and Finish Points

Middleham, with its famous castle, its strong links with the main stream of English history and its horse racing associations, straddles a hillside some two miles from Leyburn near the south bank of the River Ure. It is sited where Coverdale runs into Wensleydale. The A6108 will get you there in fine style; and once you have arrived you will find that Middleham boasts two market crosses. It is from the lower market cross that this walk begins.

Maps Needed

OS Outdoor Leisure No 30 (1:25 000)
OS Landranger No 99 (1:50 000)

Parking Facilities

They couldn't be more convenient. The lower market cross stands at the top end of a hillside parking area and there are public toilets close by.

Short Cuts

Soon after leaving Coverham the route climbs to reach Coverham Lane to point (10) before descending to recross the River Cover at Hullo Bridge. If you continue along Coverham Lane, north-eastwards, it will return you to Middleham.

An easy return from point (14) at Cover Bridge along the A6108 will reduce the distance slightly; but this road is quite busy so expect traffic.

Route Summary

The most exciting exit from Middleham is past Middleham Castle, one time home of Richard Neville, 'The King Maker', and this walk takes it. Just past the castle a short detour can be made to the site of an earlier motte and bailey castle, a must for anyone who thinks that history is more than a thing of the past. The walk continues over fields to the River Cover, which is particularly lovely hereabouts. Braithwaite Hall, Coverham Abbey and Coverham Lane, from where sweeping views lend enchantment to the walk, are all visited.

The impressive remains of the famous Middleham Castle

Then it is back to the river. From Hullo Bridge the way is now eastwards, to East Witton. The going is easy, through a delightful landscape, over level fields where all is harmony and peace and the walker has ample opportunity to commune with nature. More easy walking follows between East Witton and Cover Bridge. Leaving Cover Bridge the route edges the River Cover back upstream most delightfully for a while, then makes a sharp right turn, uphill to reach and continue along Straight Lane, leaving it close to its other end to climb across a few more fields to return to Middleham.

Interesting Features

GEOLOGY Travel up any of the main valleys of the dales and you will reach a point where arable fields give way to pasture. It is at this point that the dales landscape really begins; and in Wensleydale this happens when you cross Cover Bridge, where most of the arable land is left behind, although an occasional ploughed field may be found as far up the dale as Wensley.

Angles and Danes tended to congregate in villages where their homes and farms were grouped around open space which could be used for the safe keeping of cattle overnight and whenever danger threatened. East Witton, with its long, rectangular green, is such a village.

LANDFORMS The centrepiece of this lovely walk is the River Cover. Walking away from proud Middleham, the route is south, climbing a hillside, out of Wensleydale into Coverdale slightly to the west of a meeting of vales. Hereabouts, the countryside is particularly inviting and the River Cover at its most flattering.

Hullo Bridge, where the walk crosses the river, is built of local stone and blends delightfully with the riverside scenery. Beneath it, dark waters rush along a confining sandstone bed.

HISTORY 'Physical contact with man's habitat is essential to its history', said Hilaire Belloc and few walks illustrate it better than this one.

To anyone imbued with a sense of history this walk will pose the question; 'What sort of man was Richard III? Was he Shakespeare's deformed King or was it that over-zealous jousting and training with battle-axe and sword caused excessive development of his right arm and shoulder?' He was small of stature and there is nothing wrong with that. He was good looking and one Scottish envoy declared that he had never seen a greater mind enclosed in so small a frame. He could have spoken the truth; but it was prudent to flatter authority in those days so we cannot be certain. One thing is true though: the common people of Middleham loved him.

Today the Fellowship of the White Boar continues to fight to restore Richard's good name. It is strong in Middleham where the White Boar, Richard's heraldic emblem, still adorns the Boar Cross, one of the town's two market crosses.

Middleham Castle is concentric, built around a very large keep that dates from circa 1190 to 1200AD. A broad alleyway surrounds the keep and the other castle buildings have their outside walls built into the square curtain wall.

Coverham Bridge near the ancient remains of Coverham Abbey

Alan the Red, eldest son of Eudes, Count of Penthiere, granted Middleham to his brother, Ribold in 1086 from whom it descended through several generations to Ralph Fitzranulph, who built the Norman keep. He died without male heir in 1270 and his daughter, Mary, brought the castle, through marriage to Robert Neville.

The years between the death of their son, Ralph, in 1331, and that of the greatest of that powerful, almost royal family Richard Neville, Earl of Warwick, the King Maker, who was killed at Barnet in 1471, saw the castle's most glorious years. Following Warwick's death, the castle was forfeited to the Crown and Edward IV gave it to his brother, Richard, afterwards Richard III, who married Warwick's daughter. After Bosworth, Henry VII claimed it and it remained Crown property until James I gave it to Sir Henry Lindley in 1604.

PEOPLE Strings of horses out for their morning walks are a common sight around Middleham and lower Coverdale. Several hundred acres of the town's common fields on High Moor, Low Moor and Busks Pasture are rented to trainers. For 200 years, until 1872, a racecourse on Middleham Moor was in regular use. Today it provides splendid gallops for the 300 or so race horses locally under the care of nine or ten trainers.

Cross-Section of the Route

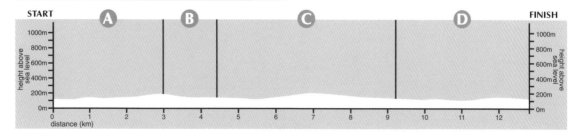

Route Description

SECTION A	2 Miles (3.2 Km)		
Destination	Braithwaite Hall (GR 118858)		
Ascent	90m(295ft)	Descent	51m(167ft)

■ **1** From the lower market cross go uphill, past the Castle Hotel, and turn left, along a cobbled pathway, between houses to Middleham Castle.

■ **2** Continue along a track, passing the castle on your right, and short of a facing gate go through a stile on your right for a detour to the motte and bailey earthworks on William's Hill. To get there cross the field, diagonally left to a gate and continue over the next field in the same direction to the castle site just ahead. Retrace your steps to the track.

■ **3** Continue up the track, through the gate and up the next field, close to a wall on your right and cross a stile in the field corner. Go down the next field close to a mix of wall and hedge on your left.

■ **4** To avoid a dip in the land go diagonally right, at a point where a wall joins the field boundary near an ash tree. Continue right, with a fence on the left, to the far bottom corner near a black hut. Turn left, over a stile, cut across the corner of a wood, exiting at another stile. Follow the clear path towards the River Cover. On reaching a bridleway sign go down a broad path to the riverbank. Go through a stile and cross the river on lovely gated Hullo Bridge.

■ **5** Ignore the footpath sign, left, and continue uphill on the clear bridleway to go through a gate. Continue climbing the next field and leave it into Hanghow Lane opposite Braithwaite Hall.

SECTION B	1 Mile (1.6 Km)		
Destination	Coverham Bridge (GR 104862)		
Ascent	0m(0ft)	Descent	29m(95ft)

■ **6** Go right, along this quiet lane, for one mile. Turn right at a T-junction, and immediately bridge the River Cover.

SECTION C	3 Miles (4.8 Km)		
Destination	East Witton (GR 142860)		
Ascent	54m(177ft)	Descent	53m(174ft)

■ **7** Take the first right, down a walled lane, passing on your right Coverham Abbey House, adjoining ruinous Coverham Abbey itself.

■ **8** At the lane end bear right, following a signpost to Pinker's Pond. Continue along a green track close to a fence on your right and go through a gate into a field. Head towards a stile at a ruinous building near the river. Cross it and take a woodland path to cross another stile. The path soon bears left, uphill as a green track. At the hilltop keep in the same direction aiming just to the left of a metal trough. Cross a stile and a beck, into a wood. Go diagonally left to a stile in a fence, leaving the wood to enter a large field. Cross it diagonally right, on rising ground, aiming for a gate and go through it.

■ **9** A minor road faces you, beyond which lies Pinker's Pond, a beautifully sited mere which is well worth a closer look. Back at point (9), go right, along the verge path, close to the fence on your right to a signpost near a seat fronting a wall.

■ **10** Go right at a gate with a bridleway sign and continue downhill on a clear green track to recross the River Cover on Hullo Bridge. Continue on the bridlepath, briefly, as far as an ash tree with the previously ignored footpath sign on it. Go sharp left along a muddy trod along the rim of the hillside, close to trees on your right. On reaching a facing wall go right, up through a gate, then diagonally left, to go through another gate. Cross this large field, bearing right to climb to the highest level, and aim for an ivy covered ash tree. Cross a footbridge, near this tree, go over a beck, beyond which, climb a stile.

■ **11** Go along the right side of the field ahead, keeping close to the hedge and about two thirds of the way along, go right, through a waymarked gate. Turn left and continue along this long field, close to the hedge now on your left. Bear right to skirt a facing fence that juts half across this field. Go forward, still with a hedge on your left and leave through a gate in a facing hedge to follow a farm track. Where it turns right, towards East Witton Lodge, go left, through a gate and immediately turn right along a clear track near a hedge on your right.

■ **12** Beyond a gateway, go ahead with the hedge on the right. At a plantation, go right at a stile, along a woodland path, exiting over a stile. Turn right, along a track that soon curves left. (A clearer path takes you around the left of the plantation to join the same track but is not a P.R.O.W.). When the track turns sharp right go ahead over a stile into a field. Cross this and the next field to go over a stile in a fence that juts out in front of you. Cross this field, up to a gate in its right-hand corner and onto a road.

SECTION D	2 Miles (3.2 Km)		
Destination	Middleham (GR 127878)		
Ascent	50m(164ft)	Descent	61m(200ft)

■ **13** Turn left, into East Witton. Just before the Methodist Chapel, go left, as signposted, with a hedge on your left. Cross a stile and continue across stiled fields with the fence now on your right. At a ruinous building go right, over a stile, edge the building on your left and go left, through a gate. Cross the next two fields to a facing gate with a footpath sign. Go across two stiled riverbank fields to a gate onto the road and cross Cover Bridge.

■ **14** Pass Cover Bridge Inn and turn left, over a stile. Follow a riverside path upstream. As hills encroach, two stiles are crossed. Continue to reach a stile going into a wood, but do not cross it.

■ **15** Turn right, uphill, to a gate into Straight Lane, an old walled track which soon becomes clearer. Continue to pass Chapel Fields Farm on the right.

■ **16** Some 100 metres past its entrance, go left at a stile. Edge the field and bear left to a stile. Cross the next field and exit at a stile into a hedged pathway to rejoin the previously used track at point (3). Retrace your steps to the start at Middleham Market Square.

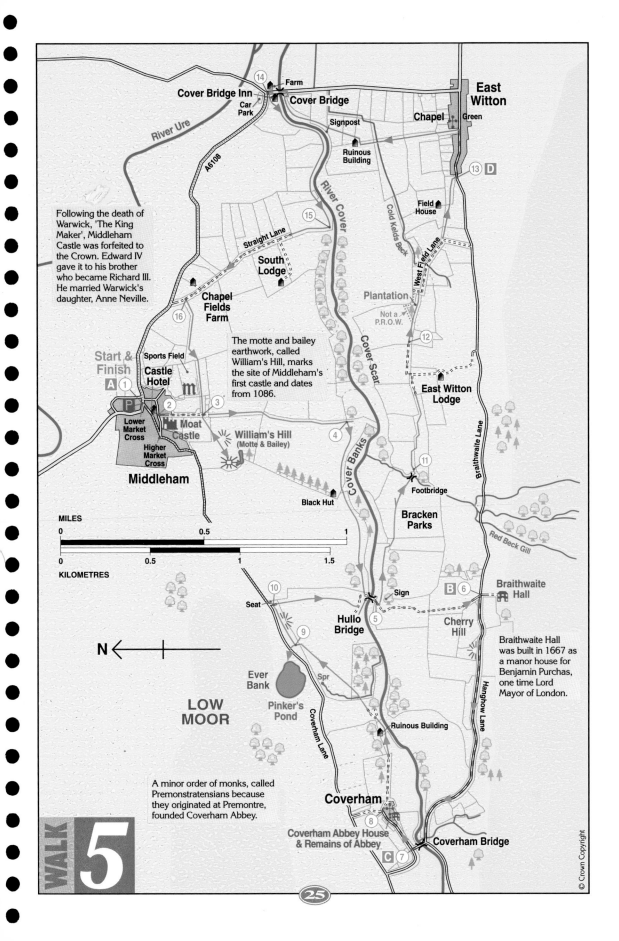

Following the death of Warwick, 'The King Maker', Middleham Castle was forfeited to the Crown. Edward IV gave it to his brother who became Richard III. He married Warwick's daughter, Anne Neville.

The motte and bailey earthwork, called William's Hill, marks the site of Middleham's first castle and dates from 1086.

Braithwaite Hall was built in 1667 as a manor house for Benjamin Purchas, one time Lord Mayor of London.

A minor order of monks, called Premonstratensians because they originated at Premontre, founded Coverham Abbey.

Cover Bridge Inn
14
Farm
Car Park
Cover Bridge
East Witton
Signpost
Chapel
Green
Ruinous Building
13 D
River Ure
A6108
River Cover
Cold Kelds Beck
Field House
15
West Field Lane
Straight Lane
South Lodge
Plantation
Not a P.R.O.W.
16
Chapel Fields Farm
12
Cover Scar
East Witton Lodge
Start & Finish
A 1
Sports Field
Castle Hotel
m
2
3
Moat Castle
William's Hill (Motte & Bailey)
4
Cover Banks
Braithwaite Lane
Lower Market Cross
11
Footbridge
Higher Market Cross
Middleham
Bracken Parks
Red Beck Gill
Black Hut

MILES
0   0.5   1

0   0.5   1   1.5
KILOMETRES

10
Seat
Sign
B 6
Braithwaite Hall
5
Cherry Hill

N

9
Hullo Bridge
Ever Bank
Spr
LOW MOOR
Pinker's Pond
Coverham Lane
Ruinous Building
Hanghow Lane

Coverham
8
7
Coverham Abbey House & Remains of Abbey
C 7
Coverham Bridge

WALK 5

WALK 6

COVER BRIDGE-EAST WITTON-ELLINGSTRING-KILGRAM GRANGE-COVER BRIDGE CIRCULAR
9.25 MILES (14.8 km)

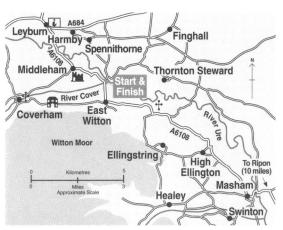

Route Details

Distance	9.25 miles (14.8 km)
Degree of Difficulty	Moderate
Ascent	150m (492ft)
Time	5.5 hours

Start and Finish Points

One mile from Middleham, in a roughly south-easterly direction, the A6108 bridges the River Cover close to where it empties into the River Ure. Adjacent to this bridge, Cover Bridge, a farm stands on one side of the road and an Inn on the other.

Here, also, at a triangular junction, a minor road branches north to cross the River Ure to the hamlet of Ulshaw and the Inn's car park stands at the road end, just across from the Inn. The walk starts here.

Maps Needed

OS Landranger No 99 (1:50 000)
OS Pathfinder No 630 (1:25 000)

Parking Facilities

Parking is limited to the nearest grass verge so an early start is advisable.

Short Cuts

Between points (8) and (9), as the apex of the walk is approached, you can cut the walking distance in half. At the road end of the farm road to Moor Cote farm, go left along a minor road that descends to the A6108.

On reaching the A6108 turn left, along it, until the entrance to Jervaulx Hall is reached, beyond where the original route is regained at point (15).

Route Summary

The first mile from Cover Bridge is across fields and not until East Witton is approached is there a hill to climb. From East Witton the way is uphill to reach the northern edge of Witton Moor.

The village of Ellingstring is reached along a quiet minor road; and it is from here that the colourful (on a clear day) descent to the lush, green valley bottom begins, followed by more pleasant walking across fields to pass below Ellington Firth Plantation and bring you to the A6108.

The solid stone arches of the Cover Bridge crossing the River Cover

Once across it, still more easy field walking lies ahead as the valley bottom is crossed and Kilgram Grange is reached. It stands close to where a minor road crosses the River Ure on an ancient and very beautiful bridge. From Kilgram Grange, the way is westwards, along the road for about half a mile to enter Jervaulx Park. A clear track takes you through parkland to join the A6108.

However, the road walking is brief. Within a short distance the A6108 is forsaken for the far superior surrounds of the River Ure where this exciting walk comes magnificently to a climax with almost two miles of glorious riverside walking.

Interesting Features

GEOLOGY Several plantations flourish on the south side of Wensleydale, touched by this walk. They overlook East Witton, Jervaulx Abbey and the now wide and increasingly arable valley bottom east of Middleham. It is a commonly held belief that the Forestry Commission concentrates almost exclusively on conifers, yet in the neighbourhood of East Witton about one seventh of the trees planted are broad leaved, mainly beech and sycamore.

Ellingstring village sits on the line which separates grazing in enclosed field pasture from rough moorland. The intakes developed during the 18th and 19th centuries when pioneers pushed their frontiers into marginal lands.

LANDFORMS Hammer farm is some 60 metres (200ft) above sea level and the smooth hill behind it rises a further 60 metres (200ft) and has, at its top, long disused Ramshaw Quarry, which is backed by a spreading plantation. A large slab of sandstone sits on the brow of the hill. The hillside is deeply grooved and well away from the farmhouse and to the east of it are more long furrows, stretching, like scratches, from higher to lower ground. For a great many years the hillside was tree covered and when they were felled many of the trees remained lying there. A few years ago the whole area was cleared and only then were the grooves exposed. The farmer, whose home is Hammer, was one of the first people to realise what had caused the grooves. They were scrape marks, made when sandstone blocks from Ramshaw Quarry were dragged by Cistercian monks to Jervaulx to be used in the building of the Abbey.

HISTORY Jervaulx Abbey began as Fors Abbey, between Askrigg and Bainbridge, but the climate was too severe and in 1156 the Cistercians moved it to its present position. Once the abbey was founded the monks set about practicing the sheep-breeding that is still an integral part of dales life. They also mined lead, burned charcoal, built the first stone walls and skillfully made Wensleydale cheese from ewe's milk to a now lost recipe. But life on the monastic estate was not always peaceful. Some of the locals resented the way the whole tracts of the country had been taken from them in particular much of the wild country in which some of the more prosperous folk had hunted. Moreover, many of the monastic officials became hard and grasping landlords, frequently dealing with tenants in ways contrary to the established customs of the manor.

The peaceful ruins of Wensleydale's Jervaulx Abbey

When the Abbot, Adam Sedburgh, died on Tyburn Hill for his part in the Pilgrimage of Grace, a mob tried to tear down the abbey. Today little more than the monastery's ground plan, five or six marble pillars that supported the chapter house and the arches that enclosed two windows on each side of the steps leading to the vanished cloister remain to enhance the scenery and imbue the place with a sense of history. That and the ghosts!

East Witton, set around a long green on which the game of quoits is played, is a quiet spot today. Yet in the 14th century it was a bustling market town. At least one of its dwellings is not all it seems. Its top windows are painted on, probably as a result of the iniquitous window tax. East Witton's present church stands proudly on elevated land at the eastern end of the village.

PEOPLE First we heard the horn, then the beagles came into view, a lively pack of perhaps twenty hounds, first rushing purposefully forward, then, having lost the hares scent, making confused circles and dashing off in a different direction. Well groomed men in green jackets and white trousers controlled the hunt, changing vantage points as the beagling proceeded, whilst in best surrealist tradition their quarry watched from almost at our feet.

Cross-Section of the Route

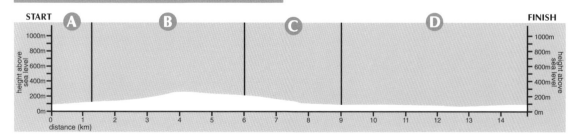

Route Description

SECTION A	1 Mile (1.6 Km)	
Destination	East Witton (GR 142860)	
Ascent	16m(52ft)	Descent 0m(0ft)

■ **1** From Cover Bridge Inn car park cross to the Inn and go left over Cover Bridge. Immediately turn right, through a gate and cross a stile, going between fence posts. Follow the path along the riverbank to cross a stile. Cross the next field to a footpath sign at a gateway. Continue diagonally right across the next two fields, aiming for a metal gate, close to a ruinous building. Turn right, edging the building on the right, to exit at a stile. Turn left, keeping to the left edge of stiled fields, to the last field with the hedge now on the right. Enter East Witton through a gate with its chapel on the left.

SECTION B	3 Miles (4.8 Km)	
Destination	Ellingstring (GR 176838)	
Ascent	134m(440ft)	Descent 40m(131ft)

■ **2** Turn left and cross the village green. On approaching the A6108 turn right, along a road with a 'No Through Road' sign which soon turns left.

■ **3** Continue along the road, soon to go between Waterloo Farm buildings and over two cattle grids.

■ **4** Climb steeply uphill towards a farmhouse, where the road becomes unsurfaced, and continue to bridge Deep Gill ending at a field.

■ **5** Here go through a waymarked gate into the field. Bear right to another waymarked gate at its top end, bending left. Continue uphill on a clear track, bearing right. At the very top of the hill go left as directed by an arrow on a gnarled ash. Turn right along the left side of a field, close to a thin wood on your left. Ignore the waymarker directing you through a break in this wood and go through a gate. Continue up the field to go through another gate, onto a farm track, where the wood ends. Go left, through a gate, beyond which, leave the main track that curves left and continue straight ahead, along a green track. Skirt a steep hill on your right, to enter Grey Yaud Plantation through a gate.

■ **6** Climb through the plantation along a forest track and on leaving it continue uphill, and go through a facing gate into a field. Go diagonally left across its corner and through a clearly seen gate onto a broad, green track that cuts across the head of a steep ravine and up through an old gate.

■ **7** Follow the green track ahead, with a plantation on the left, to reach Moor Cote Farm on your right.

■ **8** Turn right, through a gate with a footpath sign and go along a fenced track. Go through a waymarked gate into a field. Go left, close to a wall on your left and through a gateway in a facing wall. Go forward and bear left, leaving through a clearly seen gate in a wall on your left onto a driveway. Turn right, along it and through an interesting hiker's gate beside a cattle-grid and join an unsurfaced road. Go left along it, passing a plantation on your left and

nudging Witton Moor, on your right to go through a gate onto a surfaced road. Continue straight ahead, to turn left into Ellingstring village.

SECTION C	2 Miles (3.2 Km)	
Destination	Kilgram Grange (GR 191859)	
Ascent	0m(0ft)	Descent 150m(492ft)

■ **9** At the far end, just before a telephone kiosk is reached on the left, turn left down an alley, then left again at a small junction, along a lovely farm track.

■ **10** At the end of the track continue into a field and go diagonally right to go through a gate. Continue across the field ahead, slightly to the left of a large gap in the facing hedge, aiming for the left-hand side of the plantation beyond. As the land falls away into a hollow an ash tree in the facing hedge comes into view. Go through a small gate near this tree and keep in the same north-easterly direction. Continue downhill, close to a ragged hedge and keeping to the left of a depression. On reaching the bottom corner of the field go through a gate on your right. Continue along the next field close to a hedge on your left and at its far end turn left, through a metal gate onto a road, the A6108.

■ **11** Turn right along it, briefly, and where the road bends right, go left, through the first of two gates. Cross the field ahead, guided by a bridleway sign. On rounding a hillside a dead elm is clearly seen. Go through two waymarked gates beside it. The route ahead is clear and curves right, near a pond on the left, as a green track. Arrows on stones point the way. The track bears right towards Ramshaw.

■ **12** Go round the side of the building on the right to a waymarked gate, beyond which ignore a second waymarked gate across an enclosure and go left, over a stile near a beck on the right. Follow the beckside to a facing gate with a bridleway sign on it. Continue towards Kilgram Grange close to a fence on your left. On approaching the outbuildings, go through a gate, behind a hen hut. Go along a fenced path and left, through a gate, onto Kilgram Lane.

SECTION D	3.25 Miles (5.2 Km)	
Destination	Cover Bridge (GR 145871)	
Ascent	0m(0ft)	Descent 0m(0ft)

■ **13** A little detour here, right, along the lane will bring you to the medieval Kilgram Bridge, which spans the Ure. Retrace your steps and continue along Kilgram Lane, passing Lane House on your left. Where the lane turns sharp left, continue straight ahead, through a white gate, into Jervaulx Park.

■ **14** Cross this park on a clear track, first passing a pond on your right, then, on your left, Abbey Hill Farm and on your right first Jervaulx Abbey, then Jervaulx Hall to reach the A6108.

■ **15** Turn right, soon to bridge Harker Beck, beyond which turn right, through a gate, and continue down a field's edge to the River Ure. Turn left, through a gate, and continue upstream for two miles of glorious riverside walking to Cover Bridge, which you recross to return to the car park.

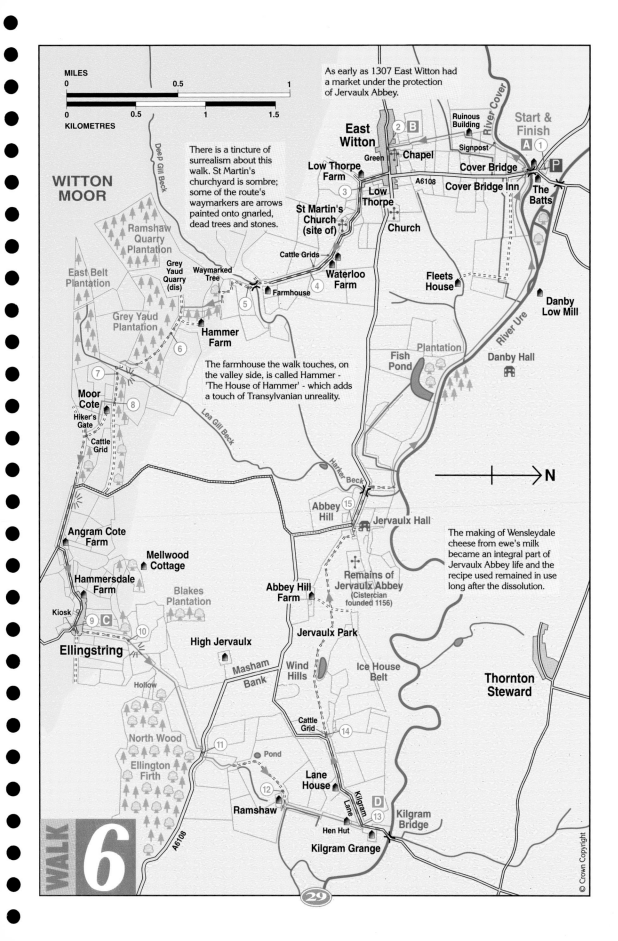

MILES

0   0.5   1

0   0.5   1   1.5

KILOMETRES

As early as 1307 East Witton had a market under the protection of Jervaulx Abbey.

WITTON MOOR

There is a tincture of surrealism about this walk. St Martin's churchyard is sombre; some of the route's waymarkers are arrows painted onto gnarled, dead trees and stones.

Deep Gill Beck

East Witton

Ruinous Building

River Cover

Start & Finish

A 1

P

Signpost

Green

Chapel

Cover Bridge

Low Thorpe Farm

A6108

Cover Bridge Inn

The Batts

3

Low Thorpe

Ramshaw Quarry Plantation

St Martin's Church (site of)

Church

East Belt Plantation

Grey Yaud Quarry (dis)

Waymarked Tree

Cattle Grids

Waterloo Farm

Fleets House

Grey Yaud Plantation

4

Farmhouse

5

Danby Low Mill

Hammer Farm

6

River Ure

Plantation

Danby Hall

The farmhouse the walk touches, on the valley side, is called Hammer - 'The House of Hammer' - which adds a touch of Transylvanian unreality.

7

Lea Gill Beck

Fish Pond

Moor Cote

8

Hiker's Gate

Cattle Grid

Harker Beck

Abbey Hill

15

Jervaulx Hall

Angram Cote Farm

Mellwood Cottage

The making of Wensleydale cheese from ewe's milk became an integral part of Jervaulx Abbey life and the recipe used remained in use long after the dissolution.

Hammersdale Farm

Blakes Plantation

Abbey Hill Farm

Remains of Jervaulx Abbey (Cistercian founded 1156)

Kiosk

9 C

10

Ellingstring

High Jervaulx

Jervaulx Park

Masham Bank

Wind Hills

Ice House Belt

Thornton Steward

Hollow

North Wood

11

Pond

Cattle Grid

14

Ellington Firth

12

Lane House

Kilgram Lane

D

A6108

Ramshaw

13

Kilgram Bridge

Hen Hut

Kilgram Grange

WALK **6**

WALK 7

CHARLES BATHURST HOTEL-WHAW MOOR-ARKLE TOWN-CHARLES BATHURST HOTEL CIRCULAR
8.5 MILES (13.6 km)

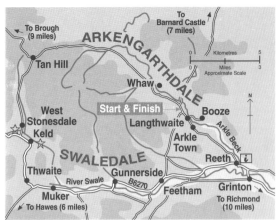

Route Details

Distance	8.5 miles (13.6 km)
Degree of Difficulty	Moderate/Strenuous
Ascent	410m (1345ft)
Time	5.5 hours

Start and Finish Points

An exciting side valley, Arkengarthdale, enters Swaledale at Reeth. From the north end of Reeth green, a road goes along it, skirting Calver Hill and descending to go through Arkle Town, which is really a hamlet. It then nudges Langthwaite, across Arkle Beck. Half a mile further up the valley from the road junction leading into Langthwaite the Charles Bathurst Hotel is reached. It stands on the right-hand side of the road and marks the start of this spectacular circular.

Maps Needed

OS Outdoor leisure No 30 (1:25 000)
OS Landranger No 92 (1:50 000)

Parking Facilities

Across the road from the Charles Bathurst Hotel there is a verge side area of flat ground where cars often park.

Short Cuts

An easy and direct escape from Turf Moor is along the minor road used to reach Bouldershaw House at point (10), which continues descending to the valley bottom and turning left to the finish.

Also, from Arkle Town, turn left at point (11) along the road for about ³/₄ mile to return you to the start of the walk.

Route Summary

The walk begins gently enough by crossing Arkle Beck before continuing upstream, to Whaw. Soon the climb begins and before long you will find yourself high on Whaw Moor, then descending to join the minor road that climbs from Feetham and descends to link with the Arkengarth road, where you are rewarded with fine views, and the back of Calver Hill is prominent ahead. From Bouldershaw House the way to Arkle Town is through rough pasture. The way out of the hamlet is across the churchyard and down a steep bank to Arkle Beck, which is crossed. A broad track continues through woodland, climbing gently, then up tilted fields, to Booze, which offers unrivalled views down Arkengarthdale.

An appealing panoramic view towards Scar House

Between Booze and Langthwaite, road walking is necessary, but is mostly steeply downhill. When the road curves left to make a direct approach to this picturesque little spot, the route continues, straight ahead, until Scar House is reached. Here, Arkle Beck is crossed once more and the track ahead is followed uphill to reach the Arkengarthdale road near the start.

Interesting Features

GEOLOGY From both the rim of Whaw Moor, to the west, and Lower Moor, to the east, the panoramic views across Arkengarthdale show why the Norse loved this little valley and settled there: it reminded them of home. They arrived from the west, from Northern Ireland, during the first quarter of the 10th century bringing a new language and establishing an Irish-Norse Kingdom that has found permanence in the origin of some of our place names and dialect.

The Anglo-Danish people had already settled on the valley bottoms when the Norse arrived; but because the Norse preferred the fells and the steep valley heads there was little clash of interest. Small groups of Celtic people were established on the uplands but mostly the land was empty and unwanted. So the Norse settled and named the natural features: fell, beck, ghyll, hill-rigg, cam, knipe, syke, slack, mere, moss, turf-moor, heath and ling which are all Norse names.

The name Arkengarthdale is derived from the Old Norse and means 'the valley of Arkill's enclosure'. Eskeleth and Langthwaite, 'the long meadow cleared from scrubland', are also Norse; but Booze, 'bower house - house by the river bend', and Whaw, 'enclosure for cows', are Old English. Arkle Town is of much later origin. It began as a miner's hovel and grew with the industry.

Mining in the North Yorkshire Dales for lead ore, which miners call galena or lead sulphide, is concentrated in Arkengarthdale, Swaledale and on the north side of Wensleydale. The veins are found mainly between 300 and 600 metres (1000 and 2000ft) and this walk passes through a broad area of disused mine workings. These mines had variable success and during the first half of the 19th century, when a severe depression hit the industry, many miners migrated to the Durham coal fields and to the Lancashire cotton towns.

LANDFORMS Arkle Beck, which springs to life on bleak Stainmore, tumbles and swirls along a stony bed on its way down the dale bottom it drains. The landscape through which it flows is a colourful mix of steep, grassy banks, wooded slopes, meadows and pastures. Wildlife abounds, flowers proliferate and the heights of Calver and Fremington Edge add a tincture of splendour. Near Reeth the Swale swallows it.

HISTORY A pub with a past marks the start of a walk with a future. The pub, now renamed the Charles Bathurst Hotel, was originally called The CB. Thereby hangs a tale and it concerns lead mining. It all began with the Romans and by the early 18th century many of the mines and associated smelt mills were on the estates of large landowners and managed by agents on their behalf. Most of the mines in Swaledale and Arkengarthdale were owned, at that time by the Whartons and these were taken over by the Denys family. In 1656 a Dr Bathurst purchased the Arkengarthdale mines and his grandson, Charles Bathurst, lord of the manor and entrepreneur, formed the CB Company which developed lead mining in the dale. Charles Bathurst's name is perpetuated in the pub's new name, the company he founded is its previous one.

The octagonal building clearly seen on higher ground to your left from the beckside field edging Stang Lane was built in 1725 as a power house. It is in a good state of preservation and its roof is intact.

An interesting view of Langthwaite village in Arkengarthdale

Langthwaite, the largest settlement in Arkengarthdale, huddles around a tiny square at a point where the valley narrows. Although its genesis is Norse, it is very much a product of the lead mining boom. It reached its zenith in the 19th century and, more recently, basked in a blaze of publicity when it was used by Walt Disney Productions as the principle setting for the film 'Escape From The Dark'.

Cross-Section of the Route

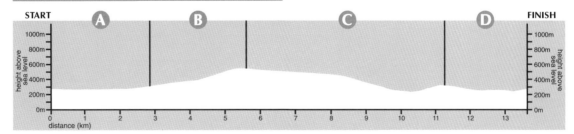

Route Description

SECTION A	1.75 Miles (2.8 Km)	
Destination	Whaw (GR 983045)	
Ascent	10m(33ft)	Descent 40m(131ft)

■ **1** From the Charles Bathurst Hotel go left southwards, briefly, and turn left into Croft House drive. Go down the drive keeping well to the left of the house and exit over a stile in the bottom left-hand corner of the grounds. Continue down the field ahead and go through a stile with a wicket in the wall on your left. Go diagonally right to another stile with a wicket in the wall on your right, beyond which you continue downhill, diagonally left to a farm road and go left along it, passing in front of West House Cottage and going through a gate onto a tarmac road close to where it bridges Arkle Beck. Turn left along this road, passing a house with kennels on your right. At a fork follow the main track, right, across a field on a farm track, leaving it to cross the tarmac road that climbs the valley side over the Stang.

■ **2** Go through a stile near a facing gate with a footpath sign and continue up the beckside. Cross a footbridge and go diagonally left across a pasture to a stile with a painted arrow. Cross it and continue across fields, upstream, to a point where another footbridge spans Arkle Beck, but do not cross it.

■ **3** Instead follow the beckside, through rocky woodland and across stiled and gated fields to reach farm buildings at Whaw hamlet.

SECTION B	3.75 Miles (6 Km)	
Destination	Bouldershaw House (GR 996018)	
Ascent	260m(853ft)	Descent 150m(492ft)

■ **4** Whaw is a delightful spot and its lovely road bridge adds to the charm. Cross this bridge and go along the surfaced road, uphill, to join the road from Reeth to Tan Hill.

■ **5** Go left, along it briefly, to go sharp right, up a signposted, unsurfaced track on your right.

■ **6** On approaching a black Nissen hut, where the track curves right, continue straight ahead and where this minor track bifurcates left, still keep ahead along what at first looks like a broad tractor track but soon becomes a green track which curves left, climbing.

■ **7** As it climbs towards the rim of Whaw Moor the faint track makes an acute right turn and soon turns left, ascending, then right, as it levels.

■ **8** On reaching a small cairn on the left turn left, leaving the clearer track that goes straight ahead. The one you are now on goes between spoil heaps in a long, gentle curve ending in a south-easterly direction and Calver is directly ahead. Where the track splits bear right through a line of grouse butts and along a clear path that soon joins a broad track at right angles. Go left along it, walking towards another line of butts clearly seen in the distance, but lower down. As you descend the track becomes clear again and, short of the butts, joins a broad,

rocky track. Continue along it passing the butts on your right and going downhill to join a minor, surfaced road.

SECTION C	1.75 Miles (2.8 Km)	
Destination	Booze (GR 015024)	
Ascent	100m(328ft)	Descent 160m(525ft)

■ **9** Turn left, along it, until Bouldershaw House Farm on your right is passed.

■ **10** Turn right towards it as directed by a footpath signpost. On nearing the farm turn left, down a rough pasture close to a wall on your right and continue beyond it in the same direction to a gate in a facing wall. Continue close to a wall on your right towards a house on your right, where a track is joined. Follow it, descending to Arkle Town.

■ **11** On reaching a minor road go right, briefly, along it towards a bridge which it crosses. Before reaching it turn left, through the hamlet. At its bottom end, where the road curves left to a dead end, go straight ahead over a stile. Cross an old churchyard along a green path to cross an extra broad stile in its bottom right-hand corner. Descend a partially stepped path to cross Arkle Beck on a footbridge at the bottom.

■ **12** Turn right along a walled lane following a path which soon enters a wood and climbs, then levels out. Where it splits take the left-hand one, climbing between trees to exit the wood at a gate and cross the field ahead, still on a clear track. At the next field leave the track and go straight ahead, briefly, following a signpost direction 'To Sleighill'. Within a few metres leave the clear, contouring path and take a fainter one on your left that climbs gradually to a gap in a facing stone wall. Go diagonally left, along the uphill path and at the top of the field go through the right-hand of two gates, crossing the next field to enter Booze through three farmyard gates.

SECTION D	1.25 Miles (2 Km)	
Destination	Charles Bathurst Hotel (GR 999031)	
Ascent	40m(131ft)	Descent 60m(197ft)

■ **13** Now follow the unsurfaced lane, left, towards Langthwaite. Soon it becomes surfaced and where it makes a sharp left turn above Langthwaite turn right along a clear path onto a wooded slope.

■ **14** With the church across the beck you have just passed, the path splits. Bear left along the lower one. Mid-way through a wood go through a wicket in a facing wall and continue. Where the path splits again, take the higher, right-hand route, uphill, which will lead you past a 'keep dogs on lead' sign behind Scar House. Join a track at right angles. Go left, downhill, to the house drive and continue right, then left, along it, to cross Arkle Beck on the bridge you were close to on the outward leg.

■ **15** Pass, for the second time, the house with the kennels only this time, where the road splits, go straight ahead on a green walled track, uphill, to the Reeth to Tan Hill road and go left, along it briefly, back to the start of this splendid walk.

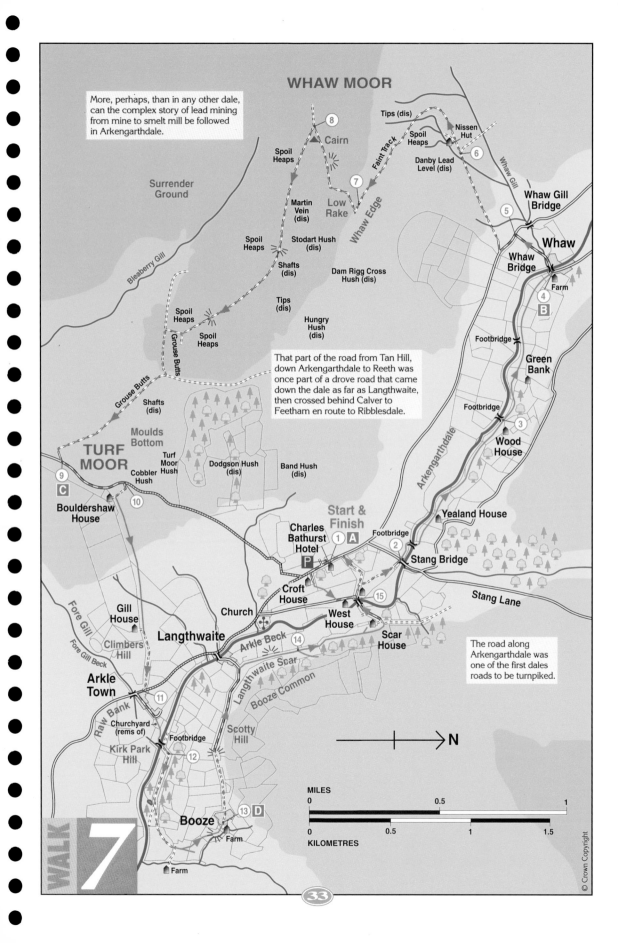

WHAW MOOR

More, perhaps, than in any other dale, can the complex story of lead mining from mine to smelt mill be followed in Arkengarthdale.

Surrender Ground

Bleaberry Gill

Spoil Heaps

8

Cairn

Spoil Heaps

Martin Vein (dis)

Stodart Hush (dis)

Spoil Heaps

Shafts (dis)

Tips (dis)

7

Low Rake

Whaw Edge

Faint Track

Tips (dis)

Danby Lead Level (dis)

Spoil Heaps

Nissen Hut

6

Whaw Gill

5

Whaw Gill Bridge

Whaw

Whaw Bridge

4 B

Farm

Dam Rigg Cross Hush (dis)

Hungry Hush (dis)

Footbridge

Green Bank

Spoil Heaps

Grouse Butts

Spoil Heaps

Grouse Butts

That part of the road from Tan Hill, down Arkengarthdale to Reeth was once part of a drove road that came down the dale as far as Langthwaite, then crossed behind Calver to Feetham en route to Ribblesdale.

Footbridge

3

Wood House

Arkengarthdale

Grouse Butts

Shafts (dis)

Moulds Bottom

TURF MOOR

Turf Moor Hush

Cobbler Hush

Dodgson Hush (dis)

Band Hush (dis)

9 C

Bouldershaw House

10

Charles Bathurst Hotel

P

Start & Finish

1 A

Footbridge

2

Stang Bridge

Yealand House

Stang Lane

Croft House

Church

Gill House

Climbers Hill

Langthwaite

West House

15

Scar House

The road along Arkengarthdale was one of the first dales roads to be turnpiked.

Arkle Beck

14

Fore Gill

Fore Gill Beck

Arkle Town

11

Churchyard (rems of)

Raw Bank

Footbridge

Kirk Park Hill

12

Langthwaite Scar

Scotty Hill

Booze Common

N

MILES
0 .... 0.5 1

0 .... 0.5 .... 1 .... 1.5
KILOMETRES

Booze

13 D

Farm

Farm

© Crown Copyright

WALK 7

8

RICHMOND-BILLY BANK WOOD-WHITCLIFFE SCAR-APPLEGARTH-RICHMOND CIRCULAR
9.5 MILES (15.2 km)

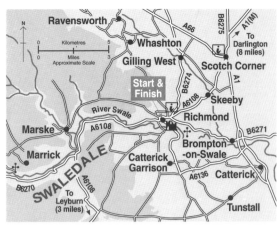

Route Details

Distance	9.5 miles (15.2 km)
Degree of Difficulty	Moderate
Ascent	170m (557ft)
Time	5.5 hours

Start and Finish Points

A pleasant, winding road, the A6108, which is famed for the number of happy holiday-makers it carries into Swaledale, will bring you through Skeeby village and into Richmond where, at the town centre roundabout, you go right, still on the A6108, pass the Georgian Theatre and turn left to reach cobbled Newbiggin Square. The walk begins and ends mid-way along this broad rectangle at a point where steep Bargate leads downhill from it.

Maps Needed

OS Outdoor Leisure No 30 (1:25 000)
OS Landranger No 92 (1:50 000)

Parking Facilities

Having turned right at the town centre roundabout, along the A6108, take the first right, briefly, to reach, on the left, a large pay-and-display car park with toilets. There are several other parking areas in Richmond, the closest to the start of the walk being in Newbiggin Square itself.

Short Cuts

From Willance's Leap, on Whitcliffe Scar, a field path leads diagonally right to join the quiet back road from Marske to Richmond close to some masts. Turn right, along it, for a pleasant, easy return to Richmond.

Route Summary

Leaving Richmond over Richmond Bridge, you are given some memorable views of its magnificent castle. Then wooded banks swallow you and the journey upstream becomes arboreal and filled with the twitterings of birds. A bridge is crossed and the climb up the north side of the valley begins. It is a pleasant climb, along a farm track and from the road at its top end the views up and down this quiet heavily wooded slice of Swaledale are very pleasing.

Looking north-west to Applegarth and Whitcliffe Scar from Hag Wood

More climbing brings you to Whitcliffe Scar and soon Willance's Leap is reached. More airy scarp top walking follows, then a short side valley, Deep Dale, is edged and the Marske to Richmond road is joined. The route follows along this quiet road, westwards in the direction of Marske, and as the road descends, a farm track to West Applegarth farm is joined. It is an easy to follow track and the route continues eastwards beyond the farm. At first it contours below, then through woodland, leaving it short of where the outward section is regained. The remainder of the walk along a minor road offers superb views and the entry into Richmond is a gentle descent.

Interesting Features

GEOLOGY As at Cover Bridge in Wensleydale, so in Swaledale, Richmond is where arable lands give way to pastures.

From the rim of the scarp above Whitcliffe Wood, panoramic views along the valley reveal that Swaledale's limestone features are limited. Only at the head of the dale, around Kidson and nearby Swinner Gill, do Swaledale's spectacular limestone features show. Unlike much of the Yorkshire Dales the valley is mostly millstone grit and this, in some measure is what gives it its special charm.

LANDFORMS Wooded Round Howe, on your left as you turn right to cross to the north side of the Swale, is a drumlin that was fortified during the Ice-Age. It has a ditch on three sides and the fourth side drops steeply to the River Swale.

HISTORY Just under Willance's Leap, between High Applegarth and Whitcliffe Wood there is an Iron-Age site that is almost complete. It consists of two or three large, square cattle enclosures protected by the high cliff to the North and a substantial rampart to the south. The remains of a dwelling with two chambers, one leading to the other is at the entrance to one of the enclosures. The site has been surveyed by the Royal Commission for Historical Monuments which consider that it was occupied by Iron-Age people up to 600 AD.

Richmond, probably the most loved town in Yorkshire, is ancient and its most redoubtable structure is its castle, said to be the oldest stone castle in England. It was founded in 1071 by Alan Rufus, Count Alan, the Red of Brittany, who was a friend of William the Conqueror's wife. At her suggestion William granted Alan Rufus many of the forfeited estates of Earl Edwin, including Richmond. He built the castle to protect the north of the country from invading Scots and to help him govern his possessions. It was magnificently sited on an eminence at the bottom of which, on the south side, the turbulent River Swale swirled. Richmond houses a 12th century church, Holy Trinity, now the regimental museum of the Green Howards, which is surrounded by a cobbled market place. Another of the town's treasures is an exquisite Georgian Theatre, the Theatre Royal. Built in 1788, this theatrical gem is the only one of that period surviving in its original form. How fitting that it should belong to Richmond which, apart from its castle and church, is very much a small Georgian town!

In 1863 something happened that could have seriously impaired Swaledale's natural beauty. A group of mine owners and lessees, hoping to get their products to the markets quickly and easily, held a meeting in Reeth, where it was proposed to form a company to build and maintain a railway up Swaledale to be known as the Richmond and Reeth Railway Company. Financial support was insufficient and the scheme was dropped.

An unusual view of the towering remains of Richmond Castle

PEOPLE In 1606 Robert Willance was hunting above Whitcliffe Scar when a thick mist came down, cutting visibility to almost nil. His horse stumbled over the 200 feet high scar, taking him with it. The horse was killed and Robert broke both of his legs but escaped with his life. He knew that in such poor conditions he had little chance of being found and that if he was not found the cold would kill him. So he cut open the body of his horse and sheltered inside it. This desperate plan saved his life though he lost one leg. The leg was buried in the churchyard and he became alderman of Richmond. Two monuments mark the site of the incident.

In 1698 Celia Fiennes 'descended a very steep hill to Richmond' and found a very large space divided into markets for fish, meat and corn. Twenty four years later Daniel Defoe visited Richmond and discovered 'all the people, great and small, knitting......and you have a market for woollen or yarn stockings'!

Cross-Section of the Route

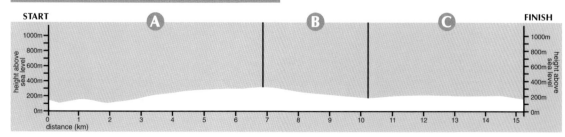

Route Description

SECTION A	4.25 Miles (6.8 Km)	
Destination	Deep Dale (GR 129024)	
Ascent	160m(525ft)	Descent 40m(131ft)

■ 1 From cobbled Newbiggin Square go southwards, down steep Bargate and continue straight ahead to cross the bridge over the River Swale and immediately turn right, into Billy Bank Wood.

■ 2 Follow a path which soon begins a gradual climb along a steep, wooded bank. Stay on this path, ignoring minor paths going from it, soon to cross a little, wooden bridge. Either go down steps to a riverside path, or keep ahead on the higher path, and continue to the edge of the wood at the foot of the bank. Both paths enter the same field at stiles close to each other.

■ 3 Continue across this level field going through gaps in broken hedges, parallel to the wooded bank on your left and the river on your right. Cross a very narrow field through a gateway and exit this small field through a clearly seen stile just ahead. Now go diagonally right, towards the river, and, keeping close to it, continue upstream to cross a signposted stile leading to a footbridge over the Swale. Once across the footbridge go straight ahead on the tarmac lane to reach the Richmond to Reeth road.

■ 4 Go left along it, and where a facing driveway joins the road at a tangent on your right, go along it.

■ 5 Turn right, uphill, along a hedged track and, near the hill top, turn first right, with the track, then left to join a farm road at right angles.

■ 6 Go left along this surfaced lane, and where it turns left to High Leases Farm, just below, keep straight ahead, through a metal gate. Turn right over a ladder-stile and climb the field ahead keeping to the left of a depression.

■ 7 On reaching a facing broken hedge at the top of the field, turn left and continue to a gateway in a wire fence at the field's corner. Keep straight ahead, at first along a faint track, then bearing left from it, aiming to meet a wall at a tangent, close to where it meets the wooded scarp top. Keep close to the fence on your left to cross a facing stile.

■ 8 Continue along the scarp top, now with a fence on your right, on a clear, stiled path to Willance's Leap, marked by two monuments and keep along the scarp top path.

■ 9 On reaching a short side valley the path curves right, still close to the scarp edge, and with a wall close to it on its right. A private surfaced road climbs steeply up this side valley and the path meets it at a cattle grid just before the back road from Richmond to Marske is reached.

SECTION B	2 Miles (3.2 Km)	
Destination	West Applegarth Farm (GR 125015)	
Ascent	0m(0ft)	Descent 118m(387ft)

■ 10 Go left along this road, towards Marske, passing Park Top Farm over on your left. The road descends past a ruined lime kiln on your left.

■ 11 Before the road descends and bends left into a side valley, fork left, off the road, and go through a metal gate. A broad, unsurfaced road is under your feet and it presents no problems. Continue along it for a scenic mile, gradually bearing round left and passing a distinctive white cairn before straightening up to reach West Applegarth Farm on your left.

SECTION C	3.25 Miles (5.2 Km)	
Destination	Richmond (GR 169009)	
Ascent	10m(33ft)	Descent 12m(39ft)

■ 12 In front of the farm, where the track bifurcates, go left as indicated by the yellow waymarker on a telegraph pole and a little further on by another arrow on a second telegraph pole and bear right, towards a clearly seen field house with a large arrow painted on it. Just before the building, go right, through a stile before a gate as the arrow indicates and then left, round the front of it and continue towards a waymarked stile, all on its own, isolated.

■ 13 From this stile cross the field ahead to a facing waymarked stile. Cross the next field to another stile behind a broken wall and cross a driveway. Go over another facing stile and climb the hill ahead, keeping to the right of a building peeping over it, slightly to your left. On going over the brow of the hill make for a stile in yet another facing wall, behind a concrete water trough. Continue over the very broad verge ahead to join the driveway to the farm on your left.

■ 14 Turn right, along it, briefly, to turn left over a stile in a wire fence. Continue down the next field, close to a wall on your left, following arrows. Keep to the left of some farm buildings and leave the field over a waymarked stile. Continue along the edge of the next enclosure keeping close to the wire fence and towards a Coast to Coast sign and join a clear farm track.

■ 15 Continue along it as it follows a course parallel to and slightly away from the foot of Whitcliffe Scar.

■ 16 When the farm track enters Whitcliffe Wood, do likewise, crossing a stile beside a closed and barbed wire-coated gate. Follow the unsurfaced, rather muddy track through the trees and exit through a wooden gate. Keep following this clear track to rejoin the route left on the outward journey above High Leases Farm.

■ 17 Go through the previously used metal gate and retrace your steps past Whitcliffe Cottage to where you first joined the road. At this point simply go straight ahead along the road, now surfaced, which will bring you back to Richmond along an ethereal route that offers excellent views of the town and that part of Swaledale. The road descends into Richmond, becoming West Fields in the process, and joins the Richmond to Reeth road on a bend.

■ 18 Keep straight ahead, towards the town centre and take the first right, into Craven Gate.

■ 19 Take the first left to return to cobbled Newbiggin, from where you started.

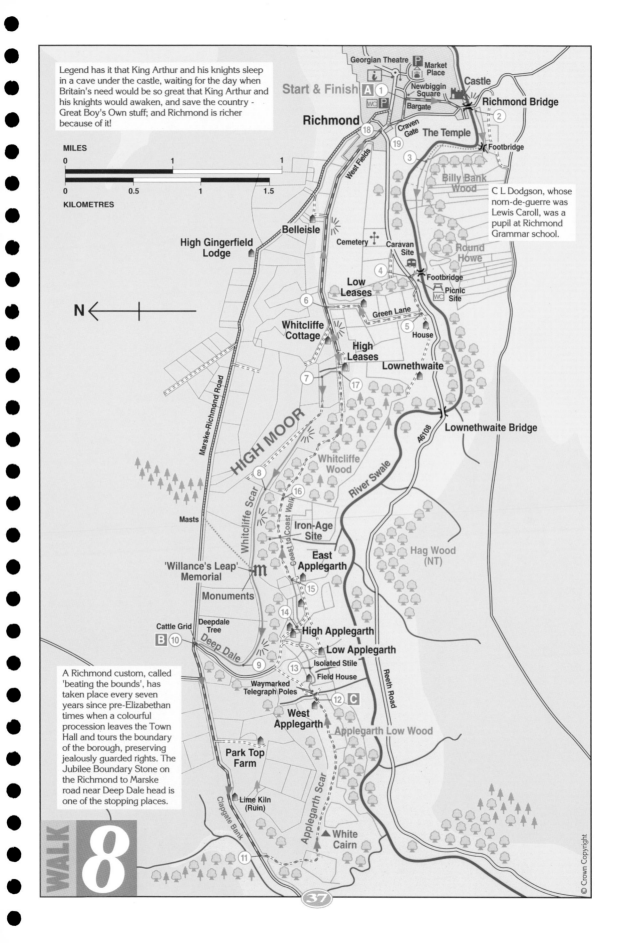

Legend has it that King Arthur and his knights sleep in a cave under the castle, waiting for the day when Britain's need would be so great that King Arthur and his knights would awaken, and save the country - Great Boy's Own stuff; and Richmond is richer because of it!

Start & Finish Ⓐ ①

Richmond

Georgian Theatre

Market Place

Newbiggin Square

Bargate

Castle

Richmond Bridge

②

Craven Gate

The Temple

Footbridge

West Fields

①⑧

⑲

③

Billy Bank Wood

C L Dodgson, whose nom-de-guerre was Lewis Caroll, was a pupil at Richmond Grammar school.

MILES

0 ⸺ 1 ⸺ 1

0 ⸺ 0.5 ⸺ 1 ⸺ 1.5

KILOMETRES

High Gingerfield Lodge

Belleisle

Cemetery

Caravan Site

Round Howe

Footbridge

Picnic Site

④

Low Leases

⑥

Green Lane

⑤

House

Whitcliffe Cottage

High Leases

Lownethwaite

N ⸺

⑦

⑰

Marske-Richmond Road

HIGH MOOR

Lownethwaite Bridge

A6108

⑧

Whitcliffe Wood

River Swale

⑯

Masts

Whitcliffe Scar

Coast to Coast Walk

Iron-Age Site

East Applegarth

Hag Wood (NT)

'Willance's Leap' Memorial

Monuments

⑮

Cattle Grid

Deepdale Tree

Ⓑ ⑩

Deep Dale

⑭

High Applegarth

Low Applegarth

Isolated Stile

⑨

⑬

Field House

⑫ Ⓒ

A Richmond custom, called 'beating the bounds', has taken place every seven years since pre-Elizabethan times when a colourful procession leaves the Town Hall and tours the boundary of the borough, preserving jealously guarded rights. The Jubilee Boundary Stone on the Richmond to Marske road near Deep Dale head is one of the stopping places.

Waymarked Telegraph Poles

West Applegarth

Applegarth Low Wood

Reeth Road

Park Top Farm

Lime Kiln (Ruin)

Clapgate Bank

Applegarth Scar

▲ White Cairn

⑪

WALK 8

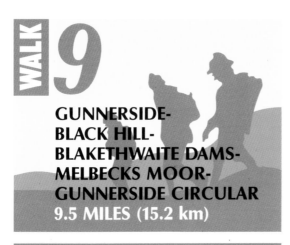

WALK 9

GUNNERSIDE-BLACK HILL-BLAKETHWAITE DAMS-MELBECKS MOOR-GUNNERSIDE CIRCULAR

9.5 MILES (15.2 km)

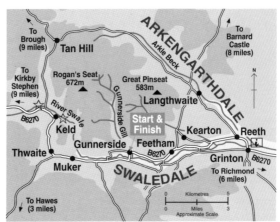

Route Details

Distance	9.5 miles (15.2 km)
Degree of Difficulty	Strenuous
Ascent	535m (1755ft)
Time	6 hours

Start and Finish Points

Swaledale is too narrow to accommodate more than one through road, the B6270, which passes through Gunnerside. As the road threads through this sturdy hamlet, going westwards, it crosses Gunnerside Beck and immediately turns left. Here, turn right to cross a car parking area that edges the beck on the right, at the far side of which stands Gunnerside Literary Institute. From it, like page one of a good book, this traveller's tale in the making, begins to unfold. Now read on.....

Maps Needed

OS Outdoor Leisure No 30 (1:25 000)

Parking Facilities

Between the Literary Institute and the bridge, spanning Gunnerside Beck, is a car park area. There are public toilets near the King's Head.

Short Cuts

From Blakethwaite Dams, a direct return to Gunnerside can be made by retracing your steps to point (8) of the route and continuing down the eastern side of Gunnerside Beck, using a clear, easy to follow path. The path is never far from the beck, crossing fields and wooded banks to arrive at Gunnerside on the B6270. Turn right, over the bridge, and right again to the start.

Route Summary

This is a tough walk, best suited to seasoned fell walkers. Without doubt, this walk is not short on the spectacular. It begins with a stiff climb onto Gunnerside Pasture where Black Hill summit is reached. Ahead, lies a steep descent into Botcher Gill and a climb out of it that will bring you to the unsurfaced track that crosses the moor from east to west. The way is right, along it.

The quaint North Yorkshire village of Gunnerside in Swaledale

Where the track curves right, it is abandoned for a descending path that descends to the bottom of the gill, from where the way to the dams is particularly exciting. The dams mark the apex of the walk. The return is back along the eastern rim of Gunnerside Gill, then there is a change, both of direction and scenery, which becomes more like a moonscape as an easterly direction is pursued. Another direction change also brings a close encounter with typical moorland scenery and for two exhilarating miles, walking along heather fringed paths and moorland tracks, the way is southwards. Contrasting with the steep climb at the start of the walk, the finish is gentle as moorland is left behind and a steep descent leads back into Gunnerside.

Interesting Features

GEOLOGY The climb along Jingle Pot Edge leads nicely to the broad heather moor that stretches northwards across the top of Gunnerside Pasture, over Black Hill and on, spreading across Hall Moor and beyond. This is red grouse country and the bird's rasping call constantly pierces the moor's brooding silence. The older, tougher heather offers shelter for them and the tender, younger shoots provide food.

Melbecks is a gritstone moor, the best kind for heather. Red grouse thrive there and from as early as February curlews begin returning to it from the coastal mud flats where they wintered, singing their bubbling song, which marks the beginning of the breeding season. It is a sound all walkers love.

LANDFORMS Of all the dales' woodland regions, those where the gills have carved sheltering ravines down the valley sides are most characteristic of the scene. The trees of which these gill woods are comprised are mostly birch shrub, mountain ash, hawthorn, holly and willow. The well-wooded part of Gunnerside Gill immediately upstream of the village is a fine example of a gill wood.

HISTORY The Norse grazed their cattle in the valleys during the spring and autumn and moved them onto the hill pastures during the summer months. The spring shieling was called a saetr, 'a pasture with houses', and Gunnerside was Gimmer's saetr. It came into being as a single Norse farm and not until many centuries later, when local lead mining increased in importance, did it grow any bigger.

On approaching Gunnerside Gill, from the rim of Lownathwaite lead mines, the degree of its involvement with lead mining becomes evident. And what an involvement!

The older mines are situated at the upper or northern end of the gill and they worked into the complex mineralisations around the Friarfold vein. Most of the levels were driven after the hillside had been 'hushed' extensively, as around Bunton Level where several large 'hushes' scar the valley side.

The methods of extracting the lead ore from the vein depended on the topography of the locality in which the mineralisation occurred. In Swaledale the most important veins lie to the north of the river and run roughly east to west. They are cut by the deep tributary valleys that enter the Swale from the north.

Some of the remains of Gunnerside Gill's lead mining history

At certain places, as near the head of Gunnerside Gill, the veins come almost to the surface and provided early prospectors with a source of ore that was relatively easy to excavate. To help in its removal the mining method of 'hushing' was used. This involved flushing the valley sides with large quantities of water to wash away the soil and loose rocks to expose the underlying rock and enable the ore to be dug from the mineralised vein. At the same time any fragments of galena that had been present in the flushed material, because of their high density would tend to be left lying on the newly exposed surface nearby. In order to collect sufficient water for the 'hushing' operation, a dam would be built near the rim of the valley, directly above the area thought to conceal a vein. It would be allowed to fill with water by collecting rain over several months or by having a stream diverted into it. When full, the dam would be breached, allowing the mass of water to rush down the valley side with such force that it cut into the surface and carried away all but the heaviest rocks. This operation was repeated several times at the same place, each scouring cutting deeper into the hillside and removing loose rocks left after ore had been cut from the vein. Galena, washed from the vein during this rush of water, would be deposited before the fragments of other rocks were, because of its density.

Cross-Section of the Route

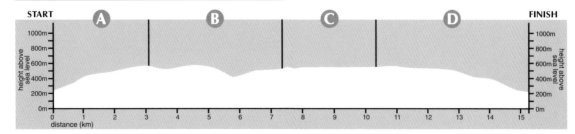

Route Description

SECTION A 2 Miles (3.2 Km)

Destination	Black Hill Summit (GR 929002)
Ascent	349m(1145ft) Descent 0m(0ft)

■ **1** From the Literary Institute, Gunnerside, go forward to the road and turn right, leaving the village between houses. Go through a small gate alongside a cattle-grid. Immediately turn right and climb steeply along a faint track that becomes clearer as it climbs. Fork sharp right, zig-zagging, partly along little sunken ways and between hawthorns, beyond which it heads straight uphill, faintly now in a north-westerly direction, passing well to the right of a building above a covered reservoir.

■ **2** When the faint trod disappears, continue in the same direction to reach an unsurfaced road that crosses your line of walk. Cross it and continue uphill on the same course. The path is undefined, then it becomes intermittent the higher it climbs up Gunnerside Pasture along Jingle Pot Edge.

■ **3** When the ground levels considerably at Knot Top, continue along a rather wet sunken path which contours and leave it when a circular stone windbreak comes into view on the left. From this windbreak, continue climbing across tussocky terrain to reach the broad summit of Black Hill.

SECTION B 2.5 Miles (4 Km)

Destination	Blakethwaite Top Dam (GR 935030)
Ascent	161m(528ft) Descent 200m(985ft)

■ **4** Go through a gate and descend northwards into a side valley. When the descent becomes almost sheer, bear left along the edge of the perpendicular bit along a narrow path that veers to the left, descending as it does so, to cross the beck in the bottom, reaching it just below a waterfall at a point where two feeders merge.

■ **5** Having crossed it, climb the steep, opposite bank and continue in a north-easterly direction to cross another feeder. Go along the foot of a bank to reach some shooting butts at an angle. Keep ahead, going over a stretch of moor that has been stripped of surface vegetation. Aim for a prominent hillock with a cairn on top, bearing left, north-westwards.

■ **6** On reaching a track go right, along it and when it bends right, turn left at a cairn, going along a green path, in-between spoil heaps, that descends steeply on reaching the top of Gunnerside Gill scarp, zig-zagging to join a broad green path.

■ **7** Turn left, downhill, to ruinous Blakethwaite Smelt Mill. Ignore the path that crosses Gunnerside Beck. It is not a P.R.O.W. and it soon peters out. Instead, continue upstream on the left bank passing a waterfall and crossing a small stream before descending to cross Gunnerside Beck.

■ **8** The path steeply climbs along the right side of the ghyll and narrows before descending to cross a small stream and climbing to reach a little plateau below the lower of the Blakethwaite Dams.

■ **9** Turn left, along this much broader route to the eastern edge of the breached wall of the lower dam. Continue climbing to the top of the wall of the higher dam, which is also breached.

SECTION C 2 Miles (3.2 Km)

Destination	Merry Field (GR 953014)
Ascent	10m(33ft) Descent 25m(82ft)

■ **10** Returning from the top dam, retrace your steps to about 400 metres before point (8) where you should see a path bearing sharply to the left. Follow this as it zig-zags steeply uphill to meet a clear track at a cairn.

■ **11** From here you could possibly detour left, back to see the site of the disused Blakethwaite lead mines. However, your return route bears right along this distinct track along the edge of Friarfold Moor. Just beyond a signpost to Keld, the track curves left to cross a moonscape-like area of spoil, guided by several cairns. After about $1/2$ mile, when the ground ahead begins to fall away, turn right through a line of shooting butts and climb a path to an old gateway in a facing wall.

SECTION D 3 Miles (4.8 Km)

Destination	Gunnerside (GR 952983)
Ascent	15m(49ft) Descent 210m(689ft)

■ **12** Keep ahead along a narrow path over rising ground in a south-easterly direction and turn left at a fork of narrow paths. The way is marked with small cairns and after $1/2$ mile it joins a track at a tangent.

■ **13** Continue right, along it, to reach some shooting butts on the left, at a junction of routes, beyond which the fine surface ends and it continues as a rough cart track. Cut through the line of shooting butts, with butt number 6 now on the right. Descend to reach a nice green area and go straight ahead, steeply downhill to a junction with a track.

■ **14** The undefined line of walk, the right of way, goes straight ahead and rejoins this track at the bottom of the slope. Turn right, along it, and just past a tip, turn left through a gate with a 'Please close the gate' sign. Continue to a stile on your left signposted 'To Low Row' and cross the field beyond it, directed by yellow dots. Leave it through a facing wicket, cross the next field, leaving through a stile, immediately stepping onto a bridge over a beck.

■ **15** Go right, along a broad green track that curves right and drops to recross this beck. On reaching a rusty gate go left, downhill, soon to curve right towards a derelict dwelling on the right.

■ **16** Just beyond it, leave the track, descending diagonally right towards a stone wall. Here, turn left to where the field funnels into a walled path. Go down this path to reach the top right-hand corner of a field. Here, turn left along a green path which joins the old corpse road, a narrow track, at a tangent.

■ **17** Turn sharp right and go steeply downhill to join a surfaced lane and go left, along it. Continue downhill to go through a gate onto the B6270. Turn left, along it, and back into Gunnerside.

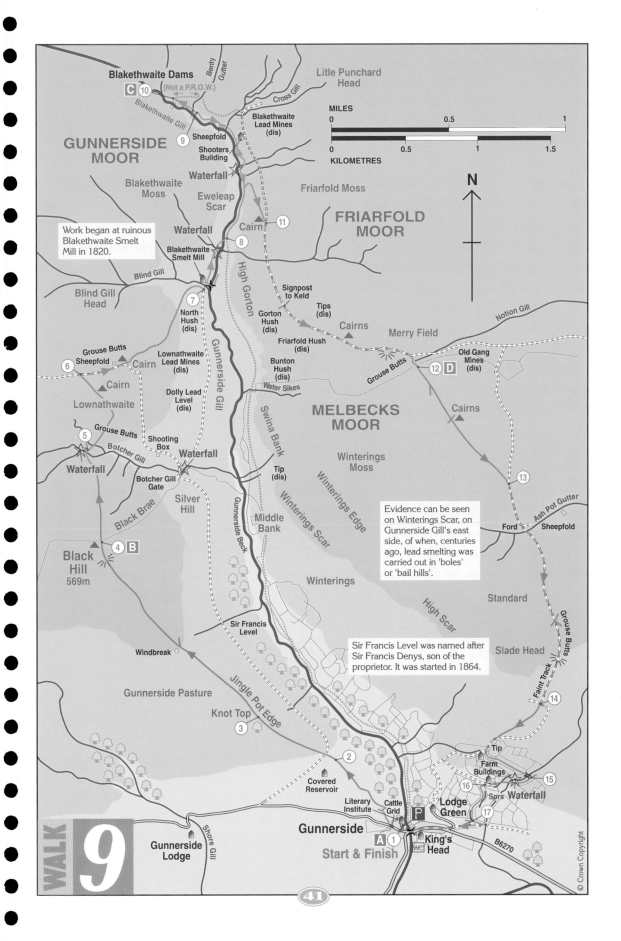

Blakethwaite Dams
C 10
(Not a P.R.O.W.)
Blakethwaite Gill
Benty Gutter
Cross Gill
Little Punchard Head
Blakethwaite Lead Mines (dis)

MILES
0   0.5   1
0   0.5   1   1.5
KILOMETRES

N

GUNNERSIDE MOOR
9
Sheepfold
Shooters Building
Waterfall
Blakethwaite Moss
Eweleap Scar
Waterfall
8
Cairn
11
Friarfold Moss

FRIARFOLD MOOR

Work began at ruinous Blakethwaite Smelt Mill in 1820.

Blakethwaite Smelt Mill
Blind Gill
Blind Gill Head
7
North Hush (dis)
High Gorton
Gunnerside Gill

Signpost to Keld
Gorton Hush (dis)
Tips (dis)
Cairns
Merry Field
Notion Gill

Grouse Butts
Sheepfold
6
Cairn
Lownathwaite Lead Mines (dis)
Cairn
Lownathwaite
Dolly Lead Level (dis)
Friarfold Hush (dis)
Bunton Hush (dis)
Water Sikes
Grouse Butts
12 D
Old Gang Mines (dis)

Cairns

5
Grouse Butts
Shooting Box
Botcher Gill
Waterfall
Waterfall
Botcher Gill Gate
Black Brae
Silver Hill
Gunnerside Beck
Middle Bank
Swina Bank
Winterings Scar
Waterfall
Tip (dis)

MELBECKS MOOR

Winterings Moss
Winterings Edge
13

Evidence can be seen on Winterings Scar, on Gunnerside Gill's east side, of when, centuries ago, lead smelting was carried out in 'boles' or 'bail hills'.

Ford
Sheepfold
Ash Pot Gutter

4 B
Black Hill
569m

Winterings
Standard
High Scar
Grouse Butts
Slade Head
Faint Track

Sir Francis Level

Sir Francis Level was named after Sir Francis Denys, son of the proprietor. It was started in 1864.

Windbreak
Gunnerside Pasture
Jingle Pot Edge
Knot Top
3
2
Covered Reservoir
Literary Institute
Cattle Grid
Gunnerside
A 1
King's Head
Start & Finish

14
Tip
Farm Buildings
15
16
Sprs
Waterfall
17
Lodge Green

Shore Gill
Gunnerside Lodge

B6270

© Crown Copyright

© Crown Copyright

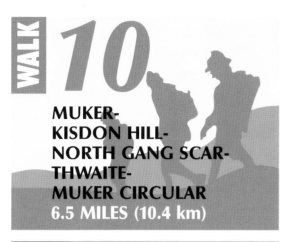

WALK 10

MUKER-KISDON HILL-NORTH GANG SCAR-THWAITE-MUKER CIRCULAR
6.5 MILES (10.4 km)

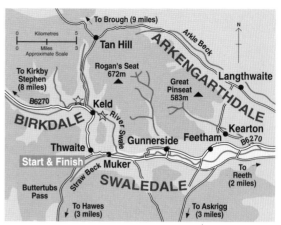

Route Details

Distance	6.5 miles (10.4 km)
Degree of Difficulty	Strenuous
Ascent	369m (1210ft)
Time	4 hours

Start and Finish Points

Muker, at the very heart of Kearton country, sits on the hem of Kisdon's skirt, alongside Straw Beck. The B6270 edges this tight cluster of dwellings on its way to Keld, at the head of Swaledale, from Gunnerside.

As this scenic road approaches Muker it runs alongside Straw Beck and bridges it at the south-eastern end of the village to continue along the beck's northern bank. If, instead of crossing this bridge, you continue straight ahead you will immediately enter a car park and it is here that this airy circular begins.

Maps Needed

OS Outdoor Leisure No 30 (1:25 000)

Parking Facilities

The pay-and-display car park lies alongside Straw Beck, on its southern bank, close to where the B6270 bridges it on reaching Muker from the east.

Short Cuts

In poor conditions, for a low level escape from high ground, stay on the track at point (8), soon to reach the B6270. Turn left, along it, to return to Muker, carefully watching out for the traffic. Having returned, by road, to Muker, cross the road bridge over Straw Beck and turn right into the car park.

Route Summary

Almost from the start you begin to climb the southern flank of Kisdon to see the full glory of Upper Swaledale unfolding like the petals of a flower warmed by the sun's rays. It is a steep climb but the views are all the sweeter because of the effort put into the climb to Kisdon's broad top.

Kisdon's western edge overlooks the original course of the River Swale, where the B6270 now runs, beyond which, in autumn, the spreading moors become a purple sea.

The youthful River Swale has sculpted the nearby Kisdon Force

Glacial action sliced through a chunk of moorland, isolating Kisdon and the resulting Kisdon Gorge, along which the Swale now flows so dramatically, spilling over splendid Kisdon Falls, is highlighted as you contour wooded Kisdon Side in the steps of the Pennine Way.

A gentler mantle is downed and the descent to Thwaite is made. Green meadows and pastures, many sporting ancient, stone-built field houses, which are as much a part of the landscape as the fields themselves, mark the return to Muker, which is approached along a lovely, flagged field path, a fine, romantic way to end this magnificent circular.

Interesting Features

GEOLOGY Before glacial pressures gouged the splendiferous limestone gorge along the eastern side of what is now Kisdon Hill, cutting it off from the main expanse of moorland, the River Swale flowed along the western side of it and developed the V-shaped valley that remains so clearly defined today.

Muker huddles at the feet of Kisdon Hill alongside Straw Beck. A cairn marks Kisdon's summit at 499m (1636ft). Its top is broad and flattish, pockmarked with sink holes, disused tips and a shaft which 'may be bottomless and could be even deeper'! The course of the walk, the right of way, sidesteps any dangerous areas and curls around the rim of its western scarp like a tail around a sleeping cat.

LANDFORMS There are few limestone features in Swaledale except around its head where the massive hulk of Kisdon and the gorge that carries the River Swale along Kisdon's eastern flank show limestone country at its most spectacular. Seen from any angle, Kisdon Hill's steep sided grandeur dominates.

HISTORY Angram, on the valley's western flank, lies at the foot of Angram Pasture. It is Norse and overlooks a landscape man-made for livestock which itself is a survival of the Norse system of husbandry.

Keld is of Norse origin and the name means 'a place near a river'. Keld Chapel, which was re-built in 1860, has a sundial dated 1840 set in its wall. The graveyard is filled with Swaledale worthies, honourable, God-fearing, hardworking dales folk, now at rest, their labours done. Alice Scott of Keldside, who died on 15th March, 1860, aged only 17 years, is among them. So is Harriet Hutchinson who, throughout her long life epitomised all the very best of dales folk characteristics.

Thwaite is also Norse and means 'a clearing'. It clusters close to Thwaite Beck, which tumbles from the heights of Great Shunner, Lovely Seat and neighbouring fells, all above 600m (2000ft).

Almost every field between Thwaite and Muker has its field house, all between 150 and 200 years old, as are the hundreds of miles of enclosure walls that lace the valley sides like weird jigsaw pieces. All the enclosure walls were built to a specification, the average height being 6 feet. The width at the base

was 3 feet tapering to 15 inches at the top. Each was really two dry-stone walls, carefully packed with small stones and there were twenty-one horizontal 'throughs' to every rood (7 yards) section. These 'throughs' bound together each section of wall. A good waller built a rood a day for which he would receive two shillings. Usually he had a boy assistant who placed the small fillings. The wallers and their assistants have all gone but the walls remain, mute testimony to their skills.

Muker began as a single Norse farm with cattle grazing the pastures closest to the farmhouse; but sheep were by far the most important stock. There were a few sheepfolds close to the farm, used mainly at lambing times, but Kisdon and other upland areas were used for most of the year. The Norse farmer moved to the high ground with the sheep during the summer months, returning to Muker after haytime.

Leaving Muker a pretty rural scene is enjoyed

PEOPLE For anyone who cares about the countryside, Muker holds special interest, for it was there that those warmly remembered naturalists, Richard and Cherry Kearton, from nearby Thwaite, went to school. Thanks to their intense interest in and devotion to wildlife and their skills, Richard with words, Cherry with a camera, they opened up a fascinating world and gave us an awareness of the need to respect and preserve the wonderful balance of Nature that has grown to become a worldwide conservation movement and made countless thousands of us armchair naturalists.

Cross-Section of the Route

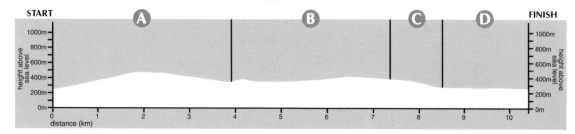

Route Description

SECTION A	2.25 Miles (3.6 Km)		
Destination	Skeb Skeugh Ford (GR 894006)		
Ascent	229m(752ft)	Descent	120m(394ft)

■ **1** From the car park, go left, over the bridge, and along the road between Muker and Straw Beck on your left. At the green triangular junction turn right, passing the Literary Institute, uphill, into the middle of the village. Pass the post office and continue forward, to Grange Farm, where you turn right, then left at a signpost, along a lane.

■ **2** Continue, along it, and on passing the last cottage on your right, go through a gate onto a steep farm road, zig-zagging upwards, through a second gate and on, still climbing.

■ **3** When it curves sharp left to a gate go straight ahead, along a green track and go through a gate. Follow a walled track and at a solitary tree, go left, towards a metal gate in a wall corner.

■ **4** Now turn right, steeply uphill with the wall on the left. Soon the way ahead becomes a wide, walled track, which narrows at a gate. Bear right at an opening along a green track, then sharp left still close to a wall on the right. Continue along a clear, broad path and through a gate in a facing wall. Go forward, at first close to the wall on your right.

■ **5** Where the wall ends, keep straight ahead on a clear path. Go through a gateway in a facing wall to enter the remains of a walled track.

■ **6** On reaching its end go straight ahead, to a gate in a facing wall. Go through the gate and straight ahead. Where the wall on the left ends continue ahead, crossing more rough pasture.

■ **7** Go through a facing gateway, to join a track that descends across gated pastures more steeply.

SECTION B	2 Miles (3.2 Km)		
Destination	Kisdon Farm (GR 903986)		
Ascent	90m(293ft)	Descent	30m(981ft)

■ **8** Where the track curves left and descends to cross Skeb Skeugh veer right, along a narrow path. Climb the hillside to go through a facing gate. Continue along a clear path, close to a wall on your left, and through another gate in a facing wall. Keep on, at first close to the wall on your left, then leaving it and passing to the right of a field house and climbing to enter a walled track. Go along it and exit through an old gate. Continue along a broad green path and go through a gateway in a facing wall.

■ **9** Bear left across the next field with the wall on the left. Exit at a sheepfold, and follow the wall on the right to meet the Pennine Way, where you turn right, along it. (Another path, bearing right from the sheepfold is used by many walkers as a safer route avoiding the cliff top, although it is not a P.R.O.W.. They contour right, across this field, cross a damp area, and continue along a winding path which becomes clearer on approaching a wall on the left at a tangent just before the Pennine Way is reached at a signpost). Continue right, along the Pennine Way.

■ **10** Almost at the end of the wood on your left cross a wall stile. Continue along Kisdon Side on a rocky path going through a mixture of gates and stiles until a stile in a fence is reached.

■ **11** Go through it and bear right on a green track to reach, on your left, a cottage and the solitary tree previously passed. Now go right, briefly, along the outward route to point (4), but now go straight ahead, along a walled track, towards Kisdon Farm.

SECTION C	1 Mile (1.6 Km)		
Destination	Thwaite (GR 894983)		
Ascent	10m(33ft)	Descent	157m(515ft)

■ **12** Go through a gate and immediately through a wooden gate to the right of a metal one. Pass Kisdon Farm on the left along a green track at the bottom of the hillside. At a 'Pennine Way' sign, turn left, as indicated, passing a field house on your right. Go through a gate in the field's corner and continue down a narrow field, passing a building built into the wall with arrows on it pointing both ways.

■ **13** Just beyond this building, where the wall on the right goes right, do likewise and cross a facing stile. Descend a cairned path to the bottom of the slope and continue along the path, close to a wall on the left. When the wall ends, the path drops diagonally left to a wall stile, going through heather.

■ **14** Go through the stile and cross the next field to reach a beck at its bottom. Go right to a metal gate and go left, through it, crossing the beck. Cross the next field, single file, as requested, along a clear path. Go through a gate and go diagonally right towards a stile entering Thwaite, but do not cross it.

SECTION D	1.25 Miles (2 Km)		
Destination	Muker (GR 911978)		
Ascent	40m(131ft)	Descent	62m(203ft)

■ **15** Go left, along the beckside and at the end of the field go through the stile, not the gate on its right. Cross the next field to another stile and keep on, passing to the left of a field house. Go over another stile in a facing wall and leave this field over another stile. Immediately go left, bridging a beck.

■ **16** Go through a facing wall stile, turn right along the field's edge and exit at a corner stile. Cross the next field to a gap between a field house and a wall. Bear left towards another stile seen to the left of an electricity post. Continue, with Straw Beck on your right, to reach the Muker to Thwaite road.

■ **17** Go left, along it, to Usha Gap farm on the left. Turn left into the farmyard and go to the right of the house to a stile to the left of a metal gate. Bear diagonally left, across this field and aim for the topmost gate in the wall on the right, but cross a stile in that wall just before the gateway is reached.

■ **18** Keeping in the same direction, close to walls on your right, cross stiled fields, to return to Muker. Leave the tarmac lane just entered by going right, down a passage to the front of the Farmer's Arms, from where you retrace your steps to the car park.

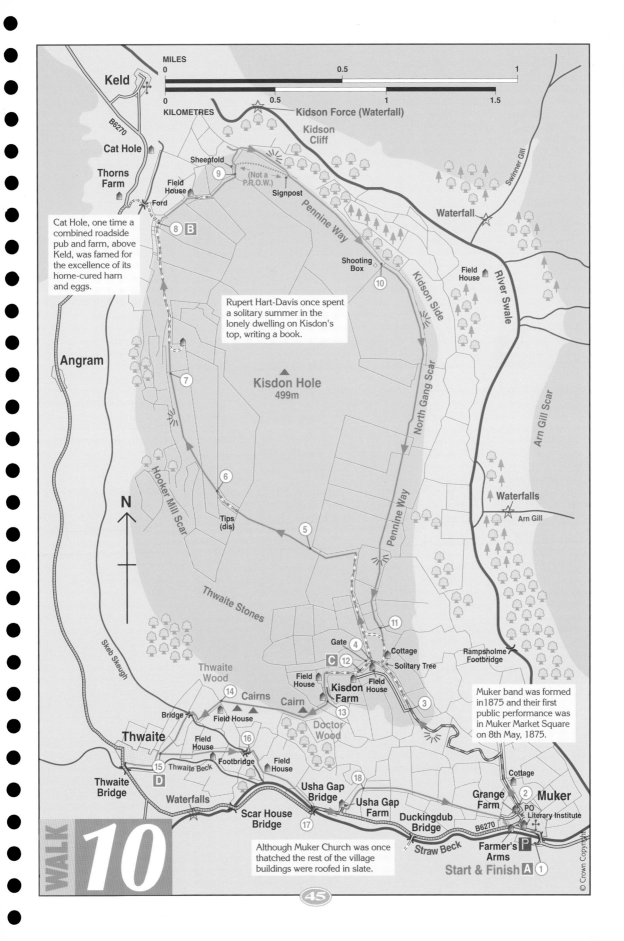

MILES
0   0.5   1

KILOMETRES
0   0.5   1   1.5

Keld

B6270

Cat Hole

Thorns Farm

Kidson Force (Waterfall)

Kidson Cliff

Sheepfold

9

(Not a P.R.O.W.)

Signpost

Field House

Ford

8 **B**

Cat Hole, one time a combined roadside pub and farm, above Keld, was famed for the excellence of its home-cured ham and eggs.

Pennine Way

Waterfall

Swinner Gill

Shooting Box

10

Kidson Side

Field House

River Swale

Rupert Hart-Davis once spent a solitary summer in the lonely dwelling on Kisdon's top, writing a book.

Angram

Hooker Mill Scar

7

North Gang Scar

Arn Gill Scar

▲ Kisdon Hole
499m

N

6

Tips (dis)

5

Pennine Way

Waterfalls

Arn Gill

Skeb Skeugh

Thwaite Stones

11

Thwaite Wood

Gate **4**

C **12**

Cottage

Solitary Tree

Rampsholme Footbridge

Field House

Kisdon Farm

Field House

3

Muker band was formed in 1875 and their first public performance was in Muker Market Square on 8th May, 1875.

14 Cairns

Cairn

13

Doctor Wood

Bridge

Field House

Thwaite

Field House

16

Footbridge

Field House

Cottage

15 Thwaite Beck

D

Thwaite Bridge

Waterfalls

Usha Gap Bridge

18

Usha Gap Farm

Duckingdub Bridge

Grange Farm

2 Muker

PO

Literary Institute

Scar House Bridge

17

Straw Beck

B6270

Although Muker Church was once thatched the rest of the village buildings were roofed in slate.

Farmer's Arms

P

Start & Finish **A** **1**

© Crown Copyright

WALK **10**

45

WALK 11

SEDBUSK-NORTH RAKES HILL-SOWRY HEAD-HARDRAW-SEDBUSK CIRCULAR

7.25 MILES (11.6 km)

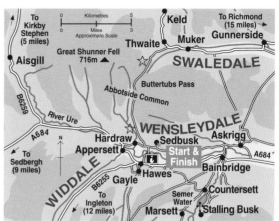

Route Details

Distance	7.25 miles (11.6 km)
Degree of Difficulty	Moderate/Strenuous
Ascent	334m (1095ft)
Time	4.5 hours

Start and Finish Points

The village of Sedbusk lies at the foot of Sedbusk High Pasture on the northern side of Upper Wensleydale, overlooking Hawes and separated from it by the River Ure.

The easiest way to get there is along either the A684 or the B6255 to Hawes, from where a minor road, Brunt Acres road, leads northwards, over the Ure, to a T-junction, from where, turn right for a short distance and take the first left, uphill, into Sedbusk, where, at a telephone kiosk near the village green, the walk begins.

Maps Needed

OS Outdoor Leisure No 30 (1:25 000)

Parking Facilities

There is limited roadside parking at the village green; but check with the locals first.

Short Cuts

From the viewpoint of Sowry Head continue downhill, along the road, which will bring you to Simonstone, from where a direct path through a succession of very narrow, stiled fields will return you to Sedbusk.

Alternatively, simply continue along the road beyond Simonstone and bear left, along Sedbusk Lane, to Sedbusk.

Route Summary

From Sedbusk a climbing lane leads up the valley side and from its top end a track leads over rough pasture to open fell. It is a steady climb and leads to an area of wild moorland. All the strenuous parts of this walk are concentrated into these moorland miles. Once the road that climbs from Wensleydale to Swaledale, over the Buttertubs Pass, is reached there is a change of direction, left, along it, for an easy descent. Here the views take over and soon the viewpoint of Sowry Head is reached. Beyond it, a short climb leads to a broad path, below which the rich, panorama of Upper Wensleydale unfolds.

The pretty green in Sedbusk village with the nearby moors beyond

From disused Stags Fell Quarries a steep descent followed by a more level crossing of fields will bring you to Simonstone, from where, as you continue downhill, over fields to Hardraw, an all enveloping, pastoral landscape is encountered; highlighting the contrast between the open fell of High Abbotside and the valley bottom. From Hardraw the Pennine Way, a flagged field path hereabouts, is followed for almost a mile and the return to Sedbusk is uphill, along field paths.

Interesting Features

GEOLOGY The sandstones of the Yoredale series are very evident around Sedbusk where quarries have yielded good building material. Pliable, workable and easily dressed to a square finish, this sandstone was used in the building of many Wensleydale houses. Today other sources have to be found because the Sedbusk quarries are worked out.

Harebells, Scottish bluebells, like dry grassy verges, even though the soil may be poor. In high summer their blue flowers nod in the breeze along the Buttertubs road, clearly happy with their lot. These same dry, green roadsides are also well suited to anyone doing this walk because soft, springy turf is far superior to a tarmac road surface.

LANDFORMS The roar of falling water heard to your right on leaving Simonstone emanates from Hardraw Force, the highest single drop waterfall in England. Access to it is through the Green Dragon. It was here, in the gorge leading to the fall, that Blondin crossed the chasm by tightrope, stopping in the middle to cook an omelette.

But Hardraw's greatest fame came between 1881 and 1929 when audiences packed the natural terraces, fashioned into rough, stone seats to listen to the bands. The gorge was acoustically pretty-near perfect and the people loved it. The renowned Black Dyke Mills Band found early fame there at a time when the Hardraw competition was considered second only to those held at Crystal Palace.

HISTORY From the airy path through Stags Fell's disused quarries Simonstone Hall catches the eye. It deserves and, since the route passes close to it, gets a closer look.

The windows of this rather splendid 18th century Manor Hall are mullioned, its chimneys stand tall and proud, as willowy and elegant as a top model. It is in fact, a credit to its proprietor, former shipping consultant, John Jeffreys and his wife, Sheila, who purchased it in 1981 when it was somewhat derelict. Using love and care and the best workmanship available he restored it to an elegant Country House Hotel. The ten bedroomed, three-crown commended hotel, when he had completed its restoration, was judged by the English Tourist Board to contain all those qualities needed to make it the bee's knees of the hotel business. These included running the kind of hotel in which the guests could hibernate for months in complete harmony. John Jeffreys was voted the warmest hotelier in all England. He was, the ETB declared, a good conversationalist and a good listener. He offered traditional English menus, roaring log fires and a friendly, smiling welcome.

Hardraw Force - England's highest single drop waterfall

PEOPLE North Rakes Hill is part of Abbotside Common, a vast area of open grazing which stretches for 10,000 acres from above Askrigg almost to Mallerstang in the Eden Valley. Open grazing on common land was once much more widespread in England than it is today. It is a system which allows several farmers to graze their stock on the high pasture and in heather. These grazing rights are keenly contested with local committees and courts deciding who shall have them. Just as there is no unrestricted access for anyone to wander on the common land, so the grazing is not unrestricted. What happens is that all the common land is stinted which means that each flock owner is allocated a certain number of sheep gaits, which vary slightly from common to common, depending on the quality and quantity of its vegetation.

On North Rakes Hill, as with all of Abbotside Common, a gait is grazing for one adult ewe or four lambs. During the summer months four ewes and their lambs constitute five parts. Grazing on this moorland landscape is an important side of the system of farming used in the dales with sheep an ever present living element.

Cross-Section of the Route

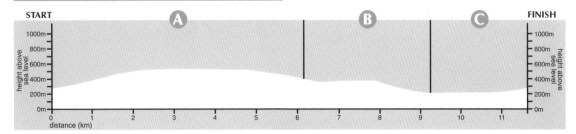

Route Description

SECTION A	3.5 Miles (5.6 Km)		
Destination	Sowry Head (GR 866928)		
Ascent	244m(801ft)	Descent	106m(348ft)

■ **1** From the telephone kiosk near Sedbusk green go uphill, northwards, and leave the village, right, along Shutt Lane that climbs steadily, passing a footpath sign 'To North Rakes Hill'. Continue along the lane, climbing steadily to reach a facing gate.

■ **2** Go left, over a ladder-stile next to a gate into a rough pasture and continue climbing along a clear, green track. Head towards a facing wall and, before reaching it, turn right along a broad, green path that goes uphill to a paddock with trees on your left, beyond which you turn left.

■ **3** The way is diagonally right, climbing along a depression to a gate in a facing wall. As it climbs, the path closes in on a wall on the right at a tangent, reaching it at a gate.

■ **4** Go through it onto open fell, bearing slightly left, along a hollow, which soon bears to the right, still climbing. At an area of sedges the land rises steeply ahead and to the right. To avoid climbing it, at first head towards it and on nearing the top of this hollow, go along a narrow, clear path towards another hollow and at a waymarked post turn left, up a clearly defined depression on a very clear, stony path to the top of the rise where there is a signpost. Here bend left, along a broad, green path that crosses the broad top of North Rakes Hill.

■ **5** When the path bifurcates take the one on the right. This clear path curves to the left to where, on the shoulder of the fell, another marker is reached. As it crosses the moorland with distant cairns to your left, the path descends gradually and bears right for a few hundred metres, then left to where it bifurcates. Here go right, along the narrower of the two. As it descends to cross an area of sedge at a land slip the path fades and is picked up again on firmer ground beyond the slip. Continue along a shallow depression sided by rocky outcrops and bear left, leaving it near its head.

■ **6** Now the first of a series of closer cairns can be seen to your left. Cross to it and follow the rim of an outcrop to the last cairn and continue ahead, passing a large, deep shake hole. Now keep in a north-westerly direction on a clear path.

■ **7** On approaching Shivery Gill bear right, round the head of a side gill and descend and cross Shivery Gill. A broad cart track is reached. Turn left, along it, to reach the Buttertubs road.

■ **8** Turn left along the road for about ³/₄ mile and cross a cattle grid with a motorists' viewing point, Sowry Head, on your right.

SECTION B	2 Miles (3.2 Km)		
Destination	Hardraw (GR 867912)		
Ascent	30m(99ft)	Descent	220m(722ft)

■ **9** From here descend along the road and where it bends right cross a ladder-stile on your left. Go straight ahead, climbing to the top right-hand corner of the field where a stile is reached.

■ **10** Cross the stile and continue along the broad path. Where it splits, curve sharp right around the base of a cairn, almost doubling back on yourself.

■ **11** Descend diagonally left to a stile in a facing wall, which you go through. Go down the field ahead, close to a wall on your right, and where it ends go diagonally right to a ladder-stile in a facing wall to the right of some sheep pens. Go over the stile and cross the next field to a gate in the far right-hand corner of a facing wall, which you go through and continue straight ahead towards farm buildings.

■ **12** Turn left, along a farm track, bearing right through a gate into the farmyard and leaving along a farm road to the main road which you cross diagonally left to a ladder-stile. Go straight ahead, through a stile to the right of a gateway. Continue along the driveway to West House Farm and turn right over a stile next to a gate.

■ **13** Turn left along a path and descend to cross a stile in a facing wall, halfway down the hillside. The path ahead starts flagged, is very distinct and goes to Hardraw. Do likewise, crossing another stile and edge a small triangular enclosure, leaving through two small gates at The Green Dragon. Go diagonally right, across the road, passing the Shepherd's Kitchen to join the Pennine Way.

SECTION C	1.75 Miles (2.8 Km)		
Destination	Sedbusk (GR 883912)		
Ascent	60m(197ft)	Descent	8m(26ft)

■ **14** Go left, along it, and within a few metres go left along a flagged path at a 'Pennine Way' footpath sign. Cross the stiled fields ahead on the flagged path to where, beyond a stile, the flags end. Here go diagonally right from the stile to a stile in the wall on your right some 20 metres to the left of a gate.

■ **15** Cross this stile, go left with the wall on your left and, where it goes left, keep ahead, aiming for a goal post. Continue in the same direction, past a flood wall, and climb a stile. You are now alongside the River Ure. Continue along the riverbank, to a facing gate, leading to the road. Turn right along it.

■ **16** Where the road bends right, cross the stile on your left, signposted 'Sedbusk 1¹/₄ mile'. Cross the field diagonally left to cross a packhorse bridge and go diagonally right, uphill and through a facing stile. Now continue climbing to the top right-hand corner, where you leave at a stile, leading to a road. Cross the road diagonally right to a stile.

■ **17** Cross the stile and fork left, going straight up the hillside on a clear path and, at the top, bear right to a stile in a wall. Cross the next narrow section of a field to a ladder-stile and go across the next one, keeping to the right of a field house and to the left of a wall that comes half way down the steep hill.

■ **18** Exit at a stile at the top right-hand corner onto a walled lane. Turn right, along it, back into Sedbusk. Turn left, past the chapel on your left, to the village green and back to the telephone kiosk.

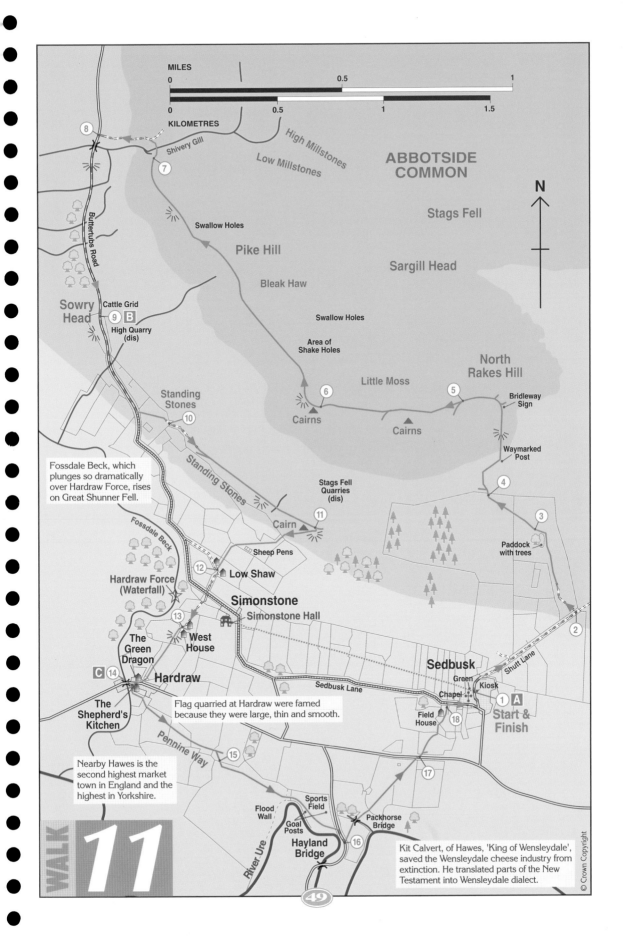

MILES
0   0.5   1

KILOMETRES
0   0.5   1   1.5

High Millstones

Low Millstones

Shivery Gill

ABBOTSIDE COMMON

Stags Fell

N

Swallow Holes

Buttertubs Road

Pike Hill

Sargill Head

Bleak Haw

Swallow Holes

Sowry Head

Cattle Grid

High Quarry (dis)

Area of Shake Holes

North Rakes Hill

Little Moss

Bridleway Sign

Standing Stones

Cairns

Cairns

Waymarked Post

Fossdale Beck, which plunges so dramatically over Hardraw Force, rises on Great Shunner Fell.

Standing Stones

Stags Fell Quarries (dis)

Paddock with trees

Fossdale Beck

Cairn

Sheep Pens

Hardraw Force (Waterfall)

Low Shaw

Simonstone

Simonstone Hall

The Green Dragon

West House

Hardraw

Sedbusk

Green

Kiosk

Sedbusk Lane

Chapel

Start & Finish

The Shepherd's Kitchen

Flag quarried at Hardraw were famed because they were large, thin and smooth.

Field House

Pennine Way

Nearby Hawes is the second highest market town in England and the highest in Yorkshire.

Sports Field

Flood Wall

Goal Posts

River Ure

Hayland Bridge

Packhorse Bridge

Kit Calvert, of Hawes, 'King of Wensleydale', saved the Wensleydale cheese industry from extinction. He translated parts of the New Testament into Wensleydale dialect.

© Crown Copyright

WALK 11

49

12

COUNTERSETT-MARSETT-STALLING BUSK-HIGH BLEAN-COUNTERSETT CIRCULAR
7.5 MILES (12 km)

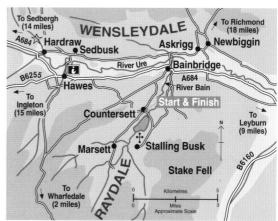

WENSLEYDALE

To Sedbergh (14 miles)
A684 Hardraw
Sedbusk
River Ure
B6255
Hawes
To Ingleton (15 miles)
Countersett
Marsett
RAYDALE
To Wharfedale (2 miles)
Askrigg
Bainbridge
A684
River Bain
Start & Finish
Stalling Busk
Stake Fell
To Richmond (18 miles)
Newbiggin
To Leyburn (9 miles)
B6160
N
Kilometres
Miles
Approximate Scale
0   5
0   3

Route Details

Distance	7.5 miles (12 km)
Degree of Difficulty	Moderate
Ascent	375m (1230ft)
Time	4.5 hours

Start and Finish Points

Countersett is a little off the beaten track. It is best reached by taking the A684 along Wensleydale to Bainbridge, from where a minor road climbs from its south-west corner.

For two snaking miles this road runs roughly parallel to the River Bain to reach Countersett, where, at a T-junction on the western edge of this quiet hamlet, the walk begins.

Maps Needed

OS Outdoor Leisure No 30 (1:25 000)

Parking Facilities

There is limited roadside parking near the T-junction at the western edge of Countersett; but check with the locals first.

Otherwise, the nearest parking area is alongside Semer Water's northern shore line between Semer Water Bridge and Little Ing's Bridge.

Short Cuts

From Marsett, just before point (6), the quiet tarmacked Marsett Lane leads directly back to Countersett, effectively cutting this glorious walk into two.

Also, just before point (12) at Low Blean Farm turn left, along the road, nudging Semer Water's northern shore to cross Semer Water Bridge and climb the steep hill ahead for a quick return to Countersett.

Route Summary

You are off to a brisk start on this one, climbing steadily for more than two miles, at first along the narrow road towards Burtersett, then crossing fields and following a steep track that continues over windswept Common Allotments. Then it is steeply downhill to Marsett from where the flat floor of Raydale is traversed and its opposite bank climbed to reach Stalling Busk.

Stalling Busk, known locally as 'Busk' is an ancient hamlet and between it and the lake is a ruinous church, built in 1603 for Semerdale.

The pretty setting of the quaint, stone-built hamlet of Countersett

A descending field path from Stalling Busk cuts through Semer Water Nature Reserve, then edges the lake before, at Low Blean Farm, the route crosses rising ground to reach surfaced Blean Lane at High Blean. Now a little road walking, left, follows until, short of High Force Farm, a change of direction is made over fields and down woodland to Low Force from where more field walking leads to the River Bain, which is followed upstream to Semer Water Bridge.

Once over the bridge, a short, steep climb along Stake Road will complete the circle.

Interesting Features

GEOLOGY Many dales change in character beyond a certain point. In Wensleydale it happens at Askrigg, which marked the end of the medieval forest. In the narrow upper dales many of the place names emanate from the Norse farmers who, during the Norman occupation, were forced to turn to keeping cows and pigs when their settlements became forest lodges and sheep grazing was restricted. Forests were wild areas, not necessarily wooded, preserved for hunting and the landlords exercised Forest Laws.

In the forest of Wensley, which extended as far as Mallerstang, lodges were established at Appersett, Burtersett, Lunds and Countersett.

Although Semer Water is a lake, Semerdale is not Lakeland. The surrounding hills are less demonstrative, more restrained, more Pennine in composition, which is as it should be for that is what they are. The outcrops are clearly limestone and, Addleborough apart, most undramatic, yet the overall effect is of harmony.

A very beautiful flower, the birds-eye primrose (primula farinosa), is only found in the wild in Cumbria and in and around Yorkshire. It loves damp, grassy places on peaty soil, all of which these slopes above Marsett provide, where it grows in some quantity.

LANDFORMS Serene Semer Water floats in a hollow of the hills, its surface mirror smooth unless stirred by angry winds. The shortest river in England, the Bain, has its birth in Semer Water; but what of the origin of the lake itself? Well, some say that glaciers scooped out the hollow in those far off ice bound ages and that little streams from Bardale, Cragdale and Raydale cut courses through the moraine and found each others company there. It is a nice story but verisimilitudinous. The truth of the matter lies in legend.

Semer Water Nature Reserve, at the head of the lake, hosts some 30 or 40 species of birds and daily, especially at nesting time, as daylight is drained from the sky, a deafening clamour shatters the stillness of the gloaming.

HISTORY The Norse grazed their cattle in the valleys during the Spring and Autumn, moving them to the hill pastures during the summer months. The spring shieling was called a saetr, 'a pasture with a house', and this element now appears as - satter, - seat - sett and - side, of which Countersett and Marsett in Semerdale are good examples.

Bronze Age people lived on the side of Semer Water which, in those days was much smaller than it is today; Iron Age people occupied the same site. In 1937, when the water level was lowered to recover a strip of marginal land, a timber structure was discovered which turned out to be a small platform set on piles at the original lakeside. A bronze spear head and some flint arrows proved that the site had been used by Bronze Age people and rings, bones of deer and pieces of iron established the site as Iron Age. For more than a thousand years the surroundings of the original lake had been occupied for most of the time.

At some point in its history the level of water rose so quickly that, indeed, lakeside dwellings were submerged. A severe cloud burst could have caused this but a more likely explanation is that a land slide blocked the lakes exit.

A panoramic view looking south-east over Semer Water,

LEGENDS Once a city stood where Semer Water now lies, and all the citizens were so selfish that when, one day, a beggar asked for alms, all refused him. Angered, he called down the wrath of heaven on its inhabitants. The rains came, the city drowned and Semer Water came into being. Today Semer Water has spread far beyond the dale, the sunken city's lack of charity is recalled in many a Northern school room.

Cross-Section of the Route

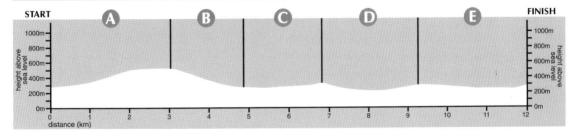

Route Description

SECTION A	2.25 Miles (3.6 Km)		
Destination	Common Allotments (GR 896874)		
Ascent	200m(656ft)	Descent	0m(0ft)

■ **1** From the T-junction on the south-east edge of Countersett go uphill, along the Burtersett road. Where the road bends sharp right go through a stile on the left marked 'Marsett Lane ¾ mile'. Cross the field ahead diagonally right, almost to the top right-hand corner and go through a stile on your right. Continue uphill, going slightly right and crossing a broken wall, aiming for a stile in the wall beyond that. Go diagonally right over a stile in the wall and immediately turn left, up the field to the ladder-stile seen earlier, which you cross onto a road.

■ **2** Go right, briefly, then left, along a track signposted 'Wetherall Fell Bridleway 2 miles'. It climbs to a gate, which you go through. Now go across a rough pasture to a gate in a wall. Continue to the top of the escarpment to reach a little stile.

■ **3** Continue straight ahead across the rough pasture and on reaching a facing gate go through it and continue across more rough pasture.

SECTION B	1 Mile (1.6 Km)		
Destination	Marsett (GR 904863)		
Ascent	0m(01ft)	Descent	235m(771ft)

■ **4** On reaching a gateway in a broken wall, turn left and begin the descent close to the wall on your right. The path here is undefined. Pull away from the wall and continue to the right of a clear water course in a depression. Now the descent steepens to reach a facing ladder-stile which you cross. Keep descending a little way from the wall on your right.

■ **5** Go through a gateway, still close to a wall on your right, and where the wall turns right, continue straight ahead aiming for a stile in a facing wall near its right-hand corner. Descend the next field to reach a farm road. Join it at the field's right-hand corner where yellow markers direct you along it to reach a surfaced road, where you turn right, into Marsett.

SECTION C	1 Mile (1.6 Km)		
Destination	Stalling Busk (GR 916858)		
Ascent	85m(279ft)	Descent	0m(0ft)

■ **6** Turn left, towards a farm and left again in front of the farmhouse. The way ahead is along a farm track which ends at a stile. Go through the stile, and keeping on the farm track, go over a field to cross Longdale Sike on a footbridge.

■ **7** Continue to cross Raydale Beck and go left, to cross a third footbridge over Cragdale Water. Bear left to cross a stile. Now turn left and go up the field ahead, aiming for a stile close to a field house but do not cross it. Instead go steeply uphill on a fading track, aiming for a telegraph pole seen ahead. Go right to the top end of the field and go through a stile in the wall on the right.

■ **8** Turn left, along a rough, walled lane to a tarmac road where you turn left along it, past a church on your right, and into Stalling Busk.

SECTION D	2 Miles (3.2 Km)		
Destination	High Blean (GR 928873)		
Ascent	40m(131ft)	Descent	90m(295ft)

■ **9** On leaving the village go left, downhill, as signposted 'Ruined Church'. Cross a cart track and go ahead along another cart track, close to a wall on your left, and where it goes left into a field, keep straight ahead, into a field. Bear left, downhill, close to a wall on your left, and where it ends, continue close to a beck on your left to a facing gate which you go through. Continue along a very clear path to the ruined church.

■ **10** From the church the path crosses stiled fields to reach Semer Water Nature Reserve and continue to a stile.

■ **11** Cross the stile and go forward, towards the Lake, soon to climb a bank and keep to the left of a field house. Continue over the next three fields to cross a road, as signposted and go through Low Blean farmyard to a gate with a yellow arrow on it.

■ **12** Continue with the beck on your right to a facing stile. Go diagonally left across a field to a stile with a yellow marker near some telegraph poles. Now cross the next field, going beneath some overhead wires, diagonally left, to reach a clear stile. Climb the steep bank ahead diagonally left, guided by a TV aerial. There is a step in the wall, which you cross into a garden.

■ **13** Go right, close to the garden wall on your right to a gate in it, which you go through. Go forward and left around High Blean on your left to enter Blean Lane.

SECTION E	1.25 Miles (2 Km)		
Destination	Countersett (GR 919878)		
Ascent	50m(164ft)	Descent	50m(164ft)

■ **14** Go left, along this surfaced lane for ⅓ mile, and on approaching High Force Farm, cross a stile with a footpath sign on the left.

■ **15** Go diagonally right, over a field, to a stile and continue in the same direction to a hollow in some trees indicated by a yellow marker at the bank's top.

■ **16** Go downhill towards Low Force Farm and cross a stile. Bear right to a farm track and through a gate into the farmyard. Turn right, climbing a lane which curves left. Just before it curves right, go left, across a route at first undefined which soon becomes a clear path to a field corner.

■ **17** Now turn left into a lane and continue close to a wall on your left. At the end of this long field go through a gate and cross the next field close to a mix of wall and hedge on your right.

■ **18** At a gate at the end of the field join another path and descend towards the River Bain on your right and continue on a stiled path to reach a road.

■ **19** Turn right, along it, over a bridge and up a very steep hill, back to Countersett, where the walk started.

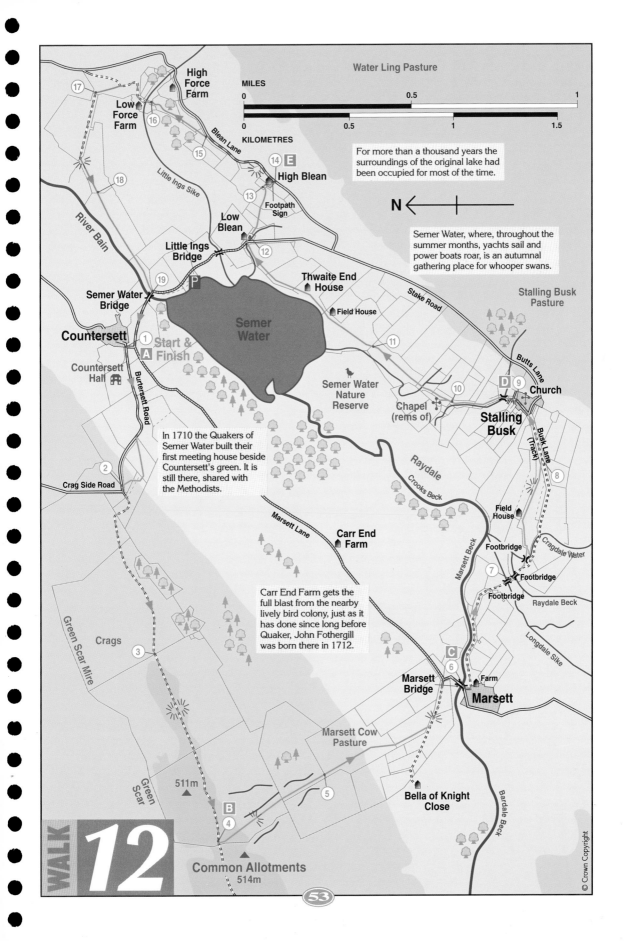

Water Ling Pasture

High Force Farm

Low Force Farm

17

16

Blean Lane

15

18

Little Ings Sike

River Bain

MILES
0   0.5   1

KILOMETRES
0   0.5   1   1.5

14 E
High Blean

13

Footpath Sign

Low Blean

Little Ings Bridge

12

19

P

Semer Water Bridge

Countersett

1
A
Start & Finish

Countersett Hall

Burtersett Road

2

Crag Side Road

For more than a thousand years the surroundings of the original lake had been occupied for most of the time.

N ←

Semer Water, where, throughout the summer months, yachts sail and power boats roar, is an autumnal gathering place for whooper swans.

Thwaite End House

Field House

Stake Road

11

Semer Water

Semer Water Nature Reserve

Chapel (rems of)

10

D 9 Church

Stalling Busk

Butts Lane

Stalling Busk Pasture

Busk Lane (Track)

8

Field House

Footbridge

7 Footbridge

Footbridge

Raydale Beck

Cragdale Water

Longdale Sike

Raydale

Crooks Beck

Marsett Beck

In 1710 the Quakers of Semer Water built their first meeting house beside Countersett's green. It is still there, shared with the Methodists.

Marsett Lane

Carr End Farm

Carr End Farm gets the full blast from the nearby lively bird colony, just as it has done since long before Quaker, John Fothergill was born there in 1712.

C
6

Marsett Bridge

Farm

Marsett

Green Scar Mire

Crags

3

Marsett Cow Pasture

5

Bella of Knight Close

Bardale Beck

Green Scar

511m ▲

B
4

Common Allotments
514m ▲

© Crown Copyright

13

REETH-BLUE HILL-DENT'S HOUSES-GRINTON-REETH CIRCULAR

14 MILES (22.4 km)

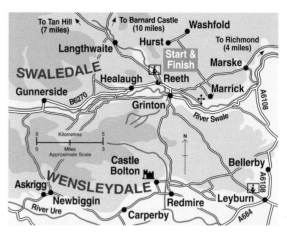

Route Details

Distance	14 miles (22.4 km)
Degree of Difficulty	Strenuous
Ascent	521m (1709ft)
Time	8 hours

Start and Finish Points

Reeth, at the very heart of Swaledale, marks the start of one of the best foot crossings from Swaledale to Wensleydale and back, using the Apedale route. Occupying a commanding position at the foot of Arkengarthdale, Reeth has become established as a dales centre of high repute. The B6270 will get you there from either up or down Swaledale while a minor road down Arkengarthdale will accommodate visitors from the north.

Hotels, pubs and cafes gather round Reeth's large green and it is from one of them, The King's Arms, that this top grade circular starts.

Maps Needed

OS Outdoor Leisure No 30 (1:25 000)

Parking Facilities

Parking facilities are available in the village of Reeth. A scale of charges is on display.

Short Cuts

If at point (5), instead of leaving a minor road above Stubbin Farm to tackle the long climb out of Swaledale, you decide to opt for a much shorter, low-level route, continue east along this road for two miles to reach point (18) at Grinton. Continue ahead and turn left, along the B6270, crossing Grinton Bridge to return to Reeth.

Route Summary

The long climb out of Swaledale begins with a descent to bridge the River Swale, from where this precocious walk at first heads towards the climbing fields ahead, then changes its mind, returns to the Swale and follows a riverside route to just upstream of Stubbin Farm. The climb towards Harker Top is much more decisive. The way is clear and the views across the valley broaden as height is gained. Then Browna Gill is crossed and the track shrinks to path size and contours through heather before climbing onto Whitaside Moor and curving southwards. Far below, that reach of the Swale south of Gunnerside is seen end on in all its U-shaped glory and this makes every upward step worthwhile.

A hazy, hot summer's day on Swaledale's purple moors

The descent of Apedale, which belongs to Wensleydale, holds no problems and the climb out of it, northwards is as clear as it is steep. From the Height of Greets the return to Swaledale begins, the valley unfolding as height is lost. Moorland falls behind as Grinton is reached and hilly pastures and lanes feature prominently between there and the swing bridge over the Swale, from where you simply retrace your steps into Reeth.

Interesting Features

GEOLOGY Disused lead mines, levels and shafts abound on Whitaside Moor, High Carl, Gibbon Hill and elsewhere across Grinton Common Pasture and along Apedale. Names like Morley's Folly evoke memories of a once thriving industry.

With its southerly neighbour Wensleydale, Swaledale was one of three major fields of lead mineralisation found in the Northern Pennines. In land area, Swaledale and Wensleydale together were considered to involve no more than one sixth of the mineralised region of the North Pennines. In terms of lead concentrates produced, their output of between 200,000 and 300,000 tonnes accounts for one twentieth of the Northern Pennines total four million tonnes.

The heather moors are high ones, reaching higher than 500m (1500ft) on the Swaledale, Wensleydale watershed. When other food is scarce in springtime sheep feed from young heather shoots, as do red grouse. To ensure a good supply of these, old heather has to be controlled by careful burning. This is a skilled operation because too much burning, too much liming or draining upsets the ecological balance and when this happens mat-grass (Nardus) takes over and it is useless as sheep food. Grouse find shelter in the older heather so care must be taken to ensure that enough of the old stuff remains for this purpose. Its spread is kept in check by grazing cattle. With sheep and grouse sharing, to some degree, the same tastes, the aims of the shepherd and the gamekeeper in moor management are similar.

LANDFORMS Extensive strip lynchets, spread along the north side of the valley are a reminder of medieval times when the Angles came as far up the dale as Healaugh, 'high clearing in a wood'. The 'laugh' part of Healaugh is Scandinavian and this place is about as far down the dale as the Norse penetrated. The strip lynchets endorse that. The Norse did not indulge in that sort of agriculture.

HISTORY An avenue of stones, laid in parallel lines, marks the entrance to Maiden Castle, which occupies an area of almost two acres of the lower slopes of Harkerside Moor. Today it is an overgrown, circular depression surrounded by a defensive mound and set atop a slope of bracken and heather. Now it is forlorn, but once, when it was a Brigantian stronghold, it was a thorn in the authority of Rome.

The Angles and the Danes tended to congregate in nucleated villages with their homes grouped around a central green on which cattle could be kept overnight or whenever danger threatened. These villages had around them a series of very small enclosures, crofts, which, along with the land actually built on, called a toft, formed a basic dwelling unit. The person living in the toft would keep one or two animals and grow a few crops in the croft, usually for domestic use only. Reeth is a good example of a toft and croft village.

Although Reeth has never quite gained the status of a small town it has become the metropolis for Upper Swaledale. From being a forest edge settlement it became the centre of farming and industry during the 18th and 19th centuries when, first, hand knitting, then lead mining brought about expansion. By the 1850s seven fairs and a weekly market were being held in Reeth. Today it has its Annual Fair at the beginning of September and its Autumn sheep sales.

The village of Reeth - the capital of Upper Swaledale

PEOPLE In the interest of efficiency, lines of butts are numbered from 1 upwards. Shooters having forked out a lot for the privilege, are allocated a certain butt number. This is standard practice throughout all grouse moors, the only exception I have come across being on Greets Hill where, instead of reading 1, 2, 3, 4, and so on, the first butt is numbered minus 0, then 0, then 1, 2, 3, 4 etc. Confusing maybe but worth 11 out of 10 for originality!

Cross-Section of the Route

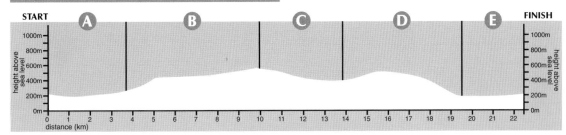

Route Description

SECTION A	2.25 Miles (3.6 Km)		
Destination	Maiden Castle (GR 018984)		
Ascent	81m(266ft)	Descent	21m(69ft)

■ **1** From The King's Arms, go right and, at the corner of the green, go right again along a lane. Bear left along a path signposted 'To the River' and continue along a lane. Turn left at a T-junction and right at the next one passing the surgery on the right. At the end of this track, turn left, on a downhill, walled path, exiting at a gate into a field, soon to cross a footbridge and bear right towards the River Swale along a clear path.

■ **2** Cross the swing bridge and go straight ahead to meet a fence on your right. As you reach a beck at the fence corner go right for a few metres and cross it. Ignore the sign to Harkerside and turn right, upstream, with a wall soon on your left. At a bridleway sign in a field corner on your right, recross the beck and cross the field diagonally left.

■ **3** On reaching the Swale, go upstream and cross a stile. Soon a blue dot on a tree is passed. Then a second blue-dotted stile is reached. Now cross a third, yellow-dotted stile and bear left up the bank as directed. Soon Stubbin Farm is passed on the left.

■ **4** Go straight ahead, following little arrows. When the wall on your left ends, bear left to a gate, guided by blue arrows. Go forward briefly, to reach a surfaced road. Go left, along it, uphill.

SECTION B	4 Miles (6.4 Km)		
Destination	Apedale Head (GR 999954)		
Ascent	287m(942ft)	Descent	5m(161ft)

■ **5** When above Stubbin Farm turn right along a bridleway, soon to reach a grouse shooters track and go right, along it. Continue on rising ground, for almost one mile, aiming for a shooters hut.

■ **6** Continue past it, as directed by the signpost to Castle Bolton. The track now becomes a grassy trod and dips and bends left to cross Browna Gill on a footbridge. It first contours the hillside, then begins a gradual climb, around the shoulder of the hillside onto an outcrop.

■ **7** Go past a ruinous lime kiln and continue along a clear, green path, passing some cairns and aiming for the head of a little gill in front of you. Continue on a narrow moorland path guided by cairns. When the path drops down into Birks Gill it cuts across a line of butts, close to the gill and a white painted marker post is passed as you continue to meet the beck near a little waterfall.

■ **8** Now cross the beck and continue parallel to the same line of butts aiming for a cairn on the horizon. As you approach it, on rising ground, a pile of stones comes into view, slightly to the right of which go to meet a line of cairns at right angles to your line of walk. Turn left, along them, towards a cairn on the horizon.

■ **9** On reaching it take the clear path to go through a broken gate and continue ahead, going to the left of a huge water-filled shaft.

SECTION C	2.25 Miles (3.6 Km)		
Destination	Dent's Houses (GR 031943)		
Ascent	0m(0ft)	Descent	170m(558ft)

■ **10** Here the way is a broad, green track bending left, then right, stretching ahead, down into Apedale. As it descends the track becomes stony.

■ **11** Bridge Jingle Pot Gill and continue downstream on a straight course, still to the left of Smithy Gill. Go through a metal gate to reach Dent's Houses.

SECTION D	3.5 Miles (5.6 Km)		
Destination	Grinton (GR 046981)		
Ascent	112m(368ft)	Descent	297m(975ft)

■ **12** On approaching a beck turn left at cross-tracks along a cart track. Stay on it, climbing for almost a mile to cross a stile in an electrified fence.

■ **13** Bear left, briefly, past a cairn to a fence and follow the clear, cairned path. Descend to meet a tarmac road at a tangent.

■ **14** Continue alongside it, and where the road bends right go left along a sunken path which soon becomes clearer and crosses a broad track.

■ **15** Go downhill to another track to the left of a white post. Turn right along it, back to the road and go left, and left again at a junction, towards Grinton.

SECTION E	2 Miles (3.2 Km)		
Destination	Reeth (GR 038993)		
Ascent	41m(134ft)	Descent	28m(92ft)

■ **16** Before reaching a road bridge, turn left at the end of a wall near a telegraph pole and go down to cross a footbridge over Grinton Gill and turn left, up a track. Where it splits go left and continue through the gate ahead, into a field. On reaching a line of electricity wires go right, close to a wall on your right and where it ends and turns right, do likewise and descend to go through a gate to the right of a barn.

■ **17** Keep going downhill to a stile, go diagonally left down the next field, aiming for a stile in the wall on your left, close to the buildings at the bottom, which you cross. Go across the next field, aiming for the big tree to the left of a white cottage. On crossing the brow of this field the stile you are seeking is clearly seen ahead in a dip in the land, in the wall on your left. Cross it, turn right, briefly, and cross a facing stile onto a tarmac road.

■ **18** Go left, along it, and where it turns left, uphill, go right, along a walled path, which leads to the Swale and, briefly alongside it. On leaving the river, continue ahead, and into a field. The clear path goes across fields keeping to the wall on the left.

■ **19** Go through two gates into a field corner and turn right. Cross the next two fields, with a fence on your right, to a stile next to a gate at the field's corner. Now continue upstream close to the Swale on your right to recross the swing bridge and retrace your steps to the start.

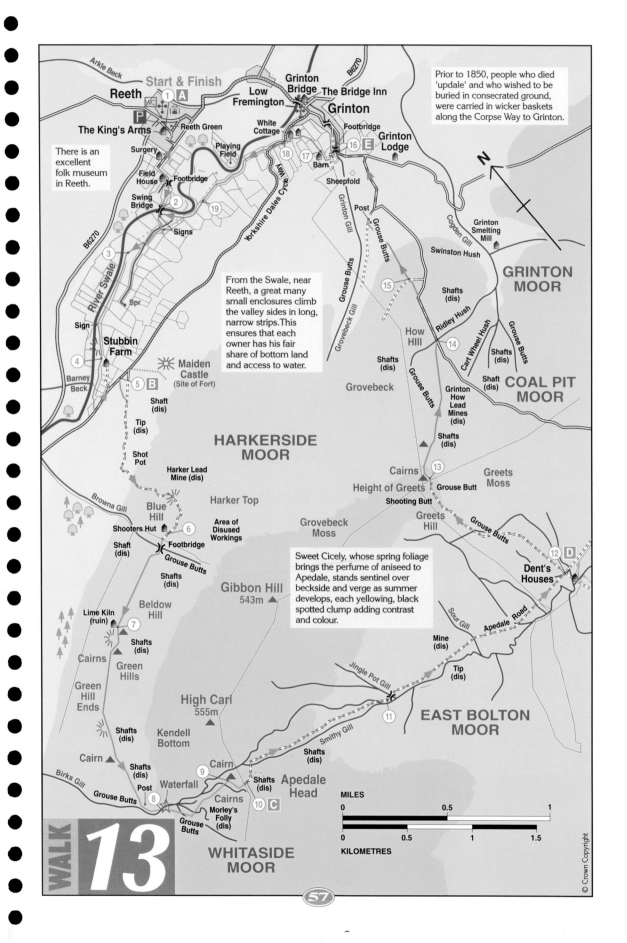

Arkle Beck

Start & Finish

Reeth ① Ⓐ
WC

The King's Arms Ⓟ

Surgery

Field House
Footbridge

Swing Bridge ②

Signs

B6270

River Swale

Spr

Sign

③

Stubbin Farm

④

Barney Beck

⑤ Ⓑ

Shaft (dis)

Tip (dis)

Shot Pot

Harker Lead Mine (dis)

Browna Gill

Shooters Hut

Blue Hill

Shaft (dis)

⑥ Footbridge

Grouse Butts

Shafts (dis)

Lime Kiln (ruin)

⑦

Shafts (dis)

Beldow Hill

Cairns

Green Hills

Green Hill Ends

Shafts (dis)

Cairn

Shafts (dis)

Birks Gill

Post

Grouse Butts

Waterfall

⑧ ⑨

Kendell Bottom

High Carl
555m

Cairn

Cairns

Morley's Folly (dis)

Shafts (dis)

⑩ Ⓒ

Grouse Butts

WHITASIDE MOOR

Gibbon Hill
543m

HARKERSIDE MOOR

Harker Top

Area of Disused Workings

There is an excellent folk museum in Reeth.

From the Swale, near Reeth, a great many small enclosures climb the valley sides in long, narrow strips. This ensures that each owner has his fair share of bottom land and access to water.

Low Fremington

White Cottage

Playing Field

Yorkshire Dales Cycle Way

⑱ ⑰

Barn

Maiden Castle
(Site of Fort)

Grinton Bridge

The Bridge Inn

Grinton

Footbridge

⑯ Ⓔ

Grinton Lodge

Sheepfold

Post

Grinton Gill

Grovebeck Gill

Grouse Butts

Grouse Butts

Grovebeck

Shafts (dis)

How Hill

⑮

⑭

Ridley Hush

Cart Wheel Hush

Cogden Gill

Swinston Hush

Grinton Smelting Mill

Shafts (dis)

Shaft (dis)

GRINTON MOOR

Shafts (dis)

Grouse Butts

COAL PIT MOOR

Grinton How Lead Mines (dis)

Shafts (dis)

Cairns

⑬

Height of Greets

Grouse Butt

Shooting Butt

Grovebeck Moss

Greets Moss

Greets Hill

Grouse Butts

Sweet Cicely, whose spring foliage brings the perfume of aniseed to Apedale, stands sentinel over beckside and verge as summer develops, each yellowing, black spotted clump adding contrast and colour.

Mine (dis)

Sour Gill

Apedale Road

⑫ Ⓓ

Dent's Houses

Jingle Pot Gill

Tip (dis)

⑪

EAST BOLTON MOOR

Smithy Gill

Shafts (dis)

Apedale Head

Prior to 1850, people who died 'updale' and who wished to be buried in consecrated ground, were carried in wicker baskets along the Corpse Way to Grinton.

N

MILES
0   0.5   1

0   0.5   1   1.5
KILOMETRES

© Crown Copyright

WALK 14

CARLTON-COTE BRIDGE-BRIDGE END FARM-FLEENSOP MOOR-CARLTON CIRCULAR

14 MILES (22.4 km)

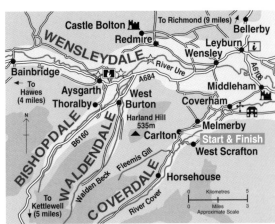

Route Details

Distance	14 miles (22.4 km)
Degree of Difficulty	Strenuous
Ascent	330m (1083ft)
Time	8 hours

Start and Finish Points

The A6108 will bring you to Middleham, from where, take a minor road, Coverham Lane, that climbs through this historic, 'horsy' spot, past its two market crosses, leaving at its south-west corner. It will bring you, in just over five miles, to Carlton where, mid-way through the village, on the south side, the Forester's Arms marks the start of this not-to-be-missed, exhilarating walk.

Maps Needed

OS Outdoor Leisure No 30 (1:25 000)

Parking Facilities

When parking in small, country places like Carlton, the views of the local inhabitants have to be considered. Otherwise it is all too easy to inadvertently obstruct someone's access. So please check your choice of parking place with the locals first. Most of the local people are only too willing to help: you will be pleasantly surprised how favourably they respond to a little consideration.

Short Cuts

You can shorten the walk by turning left, instead of right, at Whiterow Road, just before point (4), close to Cote Farm on your right. Follow this road for about a mile to rejoin the route which is about to climb to Fleensop Moor between points (8) and (9).

Route Summary

From Carlton, a climbing walled lane soon has you on Carlton Peat Moor and points you in the direction of a dip between Height of Hazely and expansive Harland Hill. Then height is quickly lost on the steep descent into the very beautiful valley of Walden Dale. The way ahead, across stiled fields on the western side of Walden Beck. The valley unfolds slowly, as though reluctant to release its secrets, as progress upstream is made. From the contouring return route the vast forest of Burton Pasture and Forelands Rigg, beyond where, Walden Dale, Bishopdale and Wensleydale all meet, are put into perspective by the sheer magnitude of the scene.

The unspoilt rural dales landscape near Carlton

When the road from West Burton, is reached, a sharp right turn leads uphill. Road walking is left behind to cross Carlton Moor. From Fleensop more field walking follows, some of it over much rougher pasture than that encountered in Walden Dale; and so the contrast is maintained throughout this carefully orchestrated exploration. It is this grand mixture of field walking along a hidden valley, first class moorland and superb views that lift this walk into a very special class.

Interesting Features

GEOLOGY Disused coal shafts abound at the head of Elm Gill, where Fleensop Colliery was sited. Despite its remoteness, Fleensop Colliery had the advantage of being placed where a thin cover of Millstone Grit allowed coal to be mined by vertical shafts sunk through the moor's surface. Coal mining was at its height there during the late 18th and early 19th centuries when it was widely used for lime burning, for those smelt mills which had the new reverberatory furnaces and for domestic use in the days before railways brought it more cheaply from outside to the dales.

Fleensop Moor is at its best when wearing autumnal purple. A good looker throughout the seasons, it is particularly beautiful in the fall.

Spring is a busy time, for it is then that heather is burned and predators like foxes and crows are controlled. General maintenance is dealt with during the summer months and autumn is the shooting season. Winter determines what happens to the moor throughout the following year. If it is a bad one with much of the heather lying under a thick cover of ice, which prevents the grouse feeding, the breeding season can be seriously affected. In a good breeding season the average brood is nine chicks and a severe winter can reduce this to nil.

Overgrazing by sheep can cause problems. Too much of it prevents natural regeneration of the heather on which the grouse feed. Heather is vulnerable. A bad year is usually followed by a worse one, which is followed by an even worse one the year after that, until the stage is reached where the plant dies and various grasses take over.

Long heather is essential as a food supply for grouse. Its tips stick out, over the snow, enabling the birds to survive the winter. Once heather reaches a certain age its growth becomes less vigorous and its food value to both grouse and sheep is diminished. This is where burning is so beneficial. It puts nutrients back into the ground and encourages a mass of new growth from seed.

Sheep should be kept on the heather moors at a level that enables them to remain as they should be - heather covered. Heather moorland is of tremendous commercial value. There is more money in grouse shooting than in sheep; and conservation is not forgotten. For if conditions are ideal for grouse they are also ideal for many other birds like curlew, snipe, lapwing, redshank, dunlin and golden plover.

LANDFORMS It is high on Buckden Pike that Waldren Beck springs to life and within the first two miles of its journey to rendezvous with first Bishopdale Beck then the Ure it has splashed and tumbled a thousand feet to reach Waldren Head. From there its course, though still lively, has lost some of its impulsiveness, though none of its charm.

Once it was called wild Waldendale and when the weather is that way out it still is. But 'wild' was also used to describe it because of its abundance of wild life. It was the last refuge in Yorkshire of the wild red deer and the pine martin. Today, unspoiled by any through road, it remains a lonely, hidden place.

The peaceful country village of Carlton in Coverdale

HISTORY As the Anglo-Saxons occupied the lower dales some of the later arrivals chose to settle in more open ground, above flood levels, where cultivation was easier. Many of these sites are indicated by the 'ton' element in their names. These 'ton' homesteads became the nuclei of small settlements. This is how Carlton came into being.

Penhill is most impressive. Near its eastern end a stone cairn marks the spot where its beacons were fired and at Nab End, on its western side, the remains of Celtic enclosures can be found.

PEOPLE Henry Constantine, the Coverdale bard lived in Carlton. His house, in the middle of the village, has a stone tablet dated 14 February 1861 and commemorates him with some pious lines.

Cross-Section of the Route

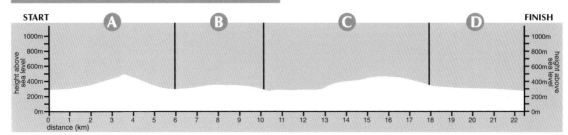

Route Description

SECTION A

SECTION A	3.75 Miles (6 Km)		
Destination	Cote Bridge (GR 018856)		
Ascent	57m(187ft)	Descent	107m(351ft)

■ 1 From the Forester's Arms, go left, through the village and where the road bends left, go straight ahead. Where this road splits, go right, along the unsurfaced one, climbing, and continue along a track onto the open moor, close to a wall on your left. A little to the left, is Howden Lodge.

■ 2 Where the wall on the left bends left, the path does likewise, going towards this building and bearing right to pass it. The track continues, first through the stoops of a gateway and then through a ruinous wall, to veer right, away from the wall on the left, soon to reach a facing gate. Go through it and continue over the brow of the hill. Descend to reach a wall on your right at a tangent. Keep close to this wall and continue along it.

■ 3 On reaching a wall, bear right, downhill towards the gill and along it. Pass a smelt mill chimney to a road, go right and cross Cote Bridge.

SECTION B

SECTION B	3 Miles (4.8 Km)		
Destination	Bridge End Farm (GR 007823)		
Ascent	70m(230ft)	Descent	60m(197ft)

■ 4 Where the road bends to the right, go left, over a stile. Go up the field and through a gated stile. Continue over stiles in a straight line for over a mile. Cross a large field with yellow markers, leaving over a stile, aiming between two ash trees. On reaching the trees the stile ahead can be seen. Go diagonally right, across a narrow field to a stile on your right.

■ 5 From here there are two paths, one a P.R.O.W., leading to Cowstone Gill House. The official route crosses both the next field and the following small triangular field diagonally right to bridge wooded Cowstone Gill.

■ 6 Edge Cowstone Gill House along a clear path and, ignoring the farm track, go straight across the field ahead to a gate. Cross the next fields to Hargill Farm. Pass the farmhouse, through a gate, cross a shallow gill and climb to a gate. Continue along the bottom of the next field to a stile. Cross the field ahead, which has a section of stone wall in it. Near the wall's top end there is a stile. Cross the stile and go over the next field, which is fenced, except in the middle, which is walled. In that wall there is a stile, which you go through. Continue to a stile, aiming for Bridge End Farm, seen ahead.

SECTION C

SECTION C	4.5 Miles (7.2 Km)		
Destination	Fleensop Farm (GR 033824)		
Ascent	193m(633ft)	Descent	93m(305ft)

■ 7 Cross the farm road and a facing stile. Bear left and descend to recross Walden Beck on a footbridge. Bear left and cross a stile in a facing wall, cross the next small field and continue diagonally right, across the next field, going up a steep bank, almost to the top right-hand corner. Turn left along the next field to a facing gate. Continue along a path, going along the bottom of a field. Go through a gate and continue above a wall, to a gate. Cross the next field to a stile. Cross the fields ahead, going over the remains of walls and at the end of the third field go through a gate. Continue over the next field, aiming for a field house ahead, on a clear track.

■ 8 Pass to the right of it and continue to Whiterow Farm, through a gap in a broken wall. On reaching the farm buildings cross a stile to reach a farm road. Go along it, in front of the farmhouse to meet a surfaced road. Turn right, to reach the hilltop and turn left at a signpost. Now climb along a track and go through a facing gate onto open fell.

■ 9 Where the path bifurcates go straight ahead. Go through a gate and continue soon to cross the head of Elm Gill, bearing right, to go through a wall, and soon to curve left to ford a beck above a waterfall. Ignoring a track going right, continue straight ahead along a climbing track, fording Coal Gill to reach a wall on the left at a tangent.

■ 10 Leave the track and go through a gateway in the wall. Go diagonally right to a wall and continue, close to it, keeping it on your right. Almost on reaching the facing wall at the far end of the field it is necessary for you to follow the P.R.O.W. by turning right to exit the field, only to turn sharp left after some 50 metres to re-enter it, although many have shown their lazy instincts and cut the corner. Descend over rough pasture, still close to the wall, to reach a plantation. Go left over a bridge, then right, over a stile and go down the next field. Bear right and soon a gate with a signpost is seen in a wall. Go through the gate and left, along a road, downhill, then climbing, towards Fleensop Farm.

SECTION D

SECTION D	2.75 Miles (4.4 Km)		
Destination	Carlton (GR 067846)		
Ascent	10m(33ft)	Descent	70m(230ft)

■ 11 Follow the lane to the right, uphill and continue ahead to go into a field. Follow a farm track bearing to the left of a building. Once past it go right across a field to a facing gate. Turn left, following the wall along two sides of the field before turning left through the wall. Immediately turn right keeping close to the wall almost reaching a wood, where you turn sharp left, drop into a hollow, climb the far side and turn sharp right to a facing stile.

■ 12 Cross the stile and over the next field to a gateway, which you go through and continue over the next field. At the far end of it descend to cross a stile, then a beck. Now cross the next field to go through a facing gate. Continue over rough pasture, going slightly left and, almost at the end of the field, bear left, through a gate in a wall on your left.

■ 13 Go diagonally right over a syke, soon reaching a gateway and continue to go through a facing gate. Now head for a farm road and continue along it, past a house on the right. The road, becoming surfaced, leads back to Carlton.

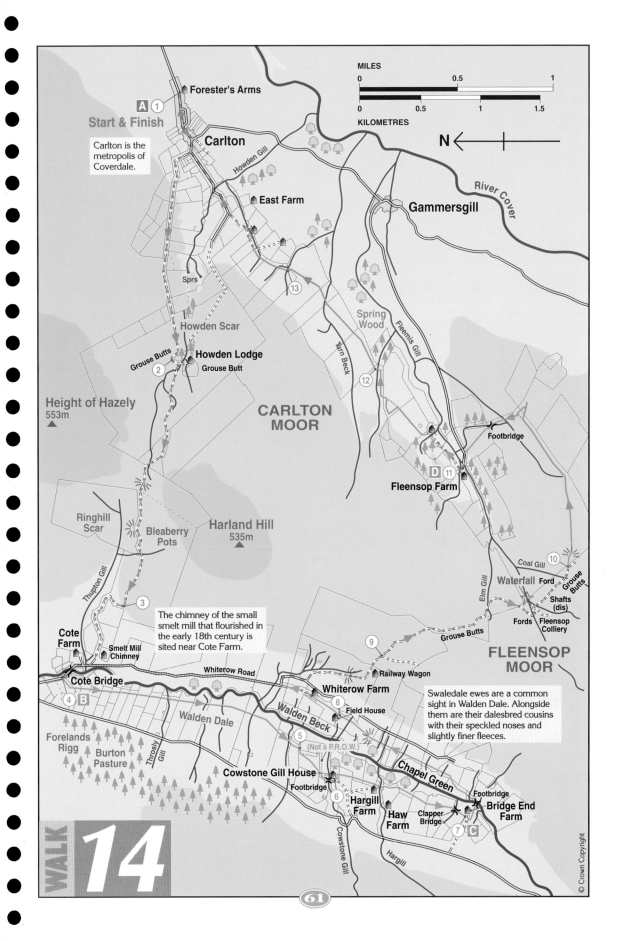

Forester's Arms

A ① Start & Finish

Carlton is the metropolis of Coverdale.

Carlton

Howden Gill

East Farm

Gammersgill

River Cover

Sprs

⑬

Howden Scar

Spring Wood

Fleemis Gill

Grouse Butts ② Howden Lodge
Grouse Butt

Height of Hazely
553m ▲

CARLTON MOOR

Turn Beck

⑫

Footbridge

D ⑪
Fleensop Farm

Ringhill Scar

Bleaberry Pots

Harland Hill
535m ▲

Coal Gill ⑩

Waterfall Ford
Grouse Butts

Thupton Gill

③

The chimney of the small smelt mill that flourished in the early 18th century is sited near Cote Farm.

Elm Gill

Shafts (dis)

Fords Fleensop Colliery

Cote Farm

Smelt Mill Chimney

Whiterow Road

⑨

Grouse Butts

FLEENSOP MOOR

Cote Bridge

Railway Wagon

Whiterow Farm

④ **B**

⑧ Field House

Walden Dale

Walden Beck

Swaledale ewes are a common sight in Walden Dale. Alongside them are their dalesbred cousins with their speckled noses and slightly finer fleeces.

Forelands Rigg

Burton Pasture

Throsty Gill

⑤
(Not a P.R.O.W.)

Chapel Green

Cowstone Gill House

Footbridge

Footbridge

⑥ Hargill Farm

Haw Farm

Clapper Bridge

Bridge End Farm

⑦ **C**

Cowstone Gill

Hargill

WALK 14

© Crown Copyright

MILES
0   0.5   1

KILOMETRES
0   0.5   1   1.5

N ←

WALK 15

THORALBY-BUSK LANE-CAUSEWAY MOSS-NEW BRIDGE-THORALBY CIRCULAR

13 MILES (20.8 km)

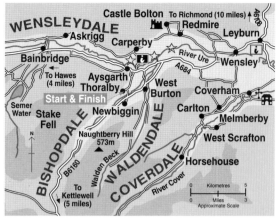

Route Details

Distance	13 miles (20.8 km)
Degree of Difficulty	Strenuous
Ascent	400m (1312ft)
Time	7.5 hours

Start and Finish Points

On approaching Aysgarth from the east, along the A684, a left-hand turn along the B6160 will bring you into Bishopdale, where in less than three miles a minor road shoots off right, briefly, to Thoralby.

Coming from the west, take the first road that leaves the A684, right, just to the east of Aysgarth. It will take you straight to Thoralby in less than a mile. Or you can use the road from Kettlewell and turn left at Cross Lanes.

Having reached Thoralby, The George Inn, on the north side of the village, is easily spotted; and it is from there that this exhilarating walk starts.

Maps Needed

OS Outdoor Leisure No 30 (1:25 000)

Parking Facilities

There is wayside parking in Thoralby, but please check with the locals first.

Short Cuts

About two miles out of Thoralby, between points (6) and (7), two paths descend left, to cross Skellicks Beck before curving left and contouring back to Thoralby.

Also, at point (16), follow the B6160 to Cross Lanes, turning left to Thoralby, thus avoiding the longer return along Bishopdale's eastern flank.

Route Summary

Resonant with promise, like a score that, from a muted beginning, swells in an exquisite crescendo, the steady climb along Haw Lane, that becomes Stake Road then an exposed moorland track, captivates the senses as height broadens the prospect and stretches horizons. It is a lonely, windswept land, this high ground of Stake Allotments, across which the walk crosses to reach walled Busk Lane. Yet, despite its remoteness, man has left his imprint, dry-stone walls being much in evidence; and there are disused lead mines on Thoralby Moor.

A pretty country lane near Thoralby in Bishopdale

The walk along Busk Lane joins the B6160 at the head of Bishopdale, at first keeping to the high ground, then dropping in steep unevenness onto the watershed. The mile of road walking that follows is hardly noticed because the road passes between dramatic scars and ahead Bishopdale unfolds. As Kidstones Bank is descended, road walking is exchanged for a pleasing contour of the valley's eastern side. Near Ribba Hall, Bishopdale Beck is recrossed, the journey continues across low lying fields and Thoralby is entered along a lane.

Interesting Features

GEOLOGY The Stake Road, a continuation of Haw Lane, which goes roughly westwards from Thoralby, leads over Stake Allotments, which when crossed in driving wind and horizontal rain, remains much as it did in 1777 when that intrepid traveller, Bray, having enthused over Aysgarth Falls, the Abbeys at Coverham and Jervaulx, Bolton and Middleham Castles, called it 'a wild and dreary moor...... at the top of which are bleak, dismal peat mosses.' What powers of observation Bray had and how accurate his description!

Dales rain soon penetrates. Flung by howling winds, it quickly drenches the wretched walker, seeping through every last stitch of clothing. But once the black udders of the clouds have been emptied and they lift, once the rain stops, dull cheerlessness becomes infused with a magical luminosity that adds sparkle to the pools and transforms Stake Allotments into a hauntingly beautiful place, as a chrysalis becomes a butterfly. Such metamorphoses are seldom seen, but once they are, treasured memory holds them.

LANDFORMS From High Scar, on Bishopdale's north-west rim, a beck cascades for a spectacular 100 metres, down the ravine of Foss Gill, while lower down the valley, at Heaning Gill, above Thoralby, more spectacular waterfalls can be found. They are an integral part of Bishopdale's hidden charms. Unfortunately, many who hasten through Bishopdale to see the famous Aysgarth Falls are unaware of these delightful cascades.

Kidstones Pass, at 425 metres (1400ft), offers a magnificent view along the full length of Bishopdale. From its brow the B6160, drops to accompany Bishopdale Beck past limestone scars and farms with date stones that show some of them to be two hundred years old while others can score three centuries.

HISTORY When the Danes began to settle with the Anglians, first in the Vale of York, then along the Pennine Valleys they sometimes infilled between existing villages and sometimes took over and renamed them. The 'by' place name element in Carperby in Wensleydale and Thoralby may represent where this took place.

Several drove roads cross the Yorkshire Dales, usually following a north to south route, but Busk Lane, joined at Stake Allotments, is not one of them. It is, in fact, one of the much more numerous market roads, which usually run east to west. Busk Lane is an exception to the rule.

The village post office and green in the rural village of Thoralby

New House was built in 1635 and is a fine example of a Pennine long house. The word 'New' in its name is a misnomer for it is the oldest house in Bishopdale.

One of the oldest inns in the dales is Street Head, which stands on the B6160 close to where a road leads into the village of Newbiggin, a little higher up the valley from Thoralby and on the opposite side of the beck. A relic of coaching times, its original oak beams are still as good as they were in 1730 when it was built.

The road on which this hostelry stands was once the only one into Newbiggin, but now there are two. The latter crosses the B6160 and continues into Thoralby, where this walk's circle is completed.

Nearby West Burton demands attention. Lying one mile to the west of Thoralby, close to the meeting of Bishopdale with Wittondale and at the foot of Penhill, it is one of the loveliest villages in Wensleydale. It's village green is one of the largest in Yorkshire and on it a tapering cross tells that this quiet spot once had a weekly market. Those days are long gone, as is the original cross. The present one was built in 1820 and restored in 1889.

Cross-Section of the Route

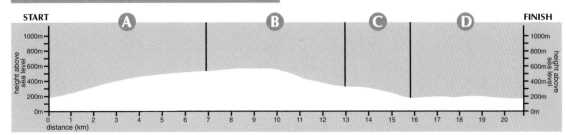

Route Description

SECTION A	4 Miles (6.4 Km)		
Destination	Busk Lane (GR 937846)		
Ascent	365m(1095ft)	Descent	0m(0ft)

■ **1** From the George Inn, Thoralby, go right, up the village, and take the first turn right, uphill.

■ **2** Curve left, out of the village, then turn sharp right to climb steadily, briefly.

■ **3** Turn left, along Haw Lane, on rising ground. From the lane Newbiggin is clearly seen across Bishopdale. After about ³/₄ mile the lane curves left.

■ **4** Cross Hacker Gill Beck before climbing to a facing gate, which you go through onto open moorland and continue close to a wall on your left.

■ **5** On reaching a gate in a facing wall, go through it. The farm clearly seen to the right and slightly ahead is Gayle Ing. Continue along a clear open track.

■ **6** Go through another gateway and on, soon to dip and go slightly left, close to a wall on the left to reach a gate in a facing wall.

■ **7** Go through it and climb steeply to a signpost at the top of the bank where you go right, following its direction.

■ **8** The track curves gently left and keeps parallel to a wall on the right. When the wall ends the track continues ahead to a gate in a facing wall.

■ **9** Beyond this wall, continue in the same direction to another gateway in a facing wall, which you go through.

■ **10** The way ahead is undefined so aim to the left of a cairn, clearly seen ahead.

■ **11** Pass the cairn and continue, bearing left towards a gateway in a facing wall near a signpost.

■ **12** Go through this gateway and along a broad track to a T-junction with Busk Lane.

SECTION B	4 Miles (6.4 Km)		
Destination	Dale Head Farm (GR 956814)		
Ascent	6m(18ft)	Descent	229m(687ft)

■ **13** Go left, along it for about two miles, crossing Stake Moss, going through areas of shake holes to reach Grey Horse Boundary Stone.

■ **14** From here, descend along Gilbert Lane, edging Cray Gill to your right and wooded Fell Pasture on your left, beyond which is Kidstones Scar. Continue to the B6160 at Causeway Moss.

■ **15** Turn left, along it, for almost a mile, beginning to descend Kidstones Bank and passing Bank Top Plantation on your left.

■ **16** On approaching Raffen Gill Plantation turn right, along a farm road, downhill, to Dale Head Farm, crossing Kidstones Beck on your way.

SECTION C	1.5 Miles (2.4 Km)		
Destination	Ribba Hall (GR 967835)		
Ascent	0m(0ft)	Descent	136m(408ft)

■ **17** Now curve left and continue across several fields on a clear track to pass Howgill.

■ **18** Continue contouring to reach a wooded gill through a gate.

■ **19** Cross this gill and continue along a clear path to enter Smelter Plantation, through a gate.

■ **20** Cross it and exit through another gate. Keeping close to the wall on your left descend as far as a waymarked stone stile in the wall on your left,

■ **21** Go through this stile, and descend the field ahead, diagonally right, to go around the side of Smelter Farm onto a farm road.

■ **22** Turn left, along it, briefly, to go right and head towards a gateway.

■ **23** Go through the gateway and continue past Myers Garth and towards Ribba Hall, both on your right.

SECTION D	3.5 Miles (5.6 Km)		
Destination	Thoralby (GR 000868)		
Ascent	29m(87ft)	Descent	35m(105ft)

■ **24** Once past Ribba Hall go along a short farm road that crosses Bishopdale Beck. The farmer at Ribba would like you to use this route, with his blessing, so that you spend as short a time on his land as possible. But the correct route is through a gate near the bridge and along the riverside for ¹/₅ mile to exit onto the B6160 at New Bridge. Go left along the road, crossing Bishopdale Beck, and passing the bridge from Ribba Hall on your left.

■ **25** At a junction, go right, along the farm road to reach New House Farm.

■ **26** Turn right, in front of it and cross the field ahead to a stile, the first in a series leading to Thoralby.

■ **27** Keeping in the same direction, crossing fields, the route edges Faw Wood and Odlin Holes Wood on your left. As each field is reached at a wall stile, the stile at the far end of it is seen.

■ **28** When Howesyke Farm is seen ahead, slightly to the right, aim for the far end of a modern outhouse, which has a directional arrow painted on it.

■ **29** At the end of this building go through a gate on the right, down the side of it, through another gate and left, leaving the farm along a farm road.

■ **30** Leave this farm road to go diagonally right to a wall stile in a facing wall.

■ **31** Go through the stile and continue ahead, crossing the farm road which has turned right to cross your line of walk.

■ **32** Cross a stile in a facing wall, go over the next field and leave it over another wall stile close to Crooksby Barn on the left.

■ **33** Keeping in the same direction continue over stiled fields to join Westfield Lane.

■ **34** Follow this lane soon to nudge Bishopdale Beck on your right, as it meanders.

■ **35** Continue to cross Swinacote Gill on Littleburn Bridge soon to reach the western edge of Thoralby.

■ **36** Turn right at a T-junction and continue along the village to The George Inn, ready, perhaps, for a pint following your exertions.

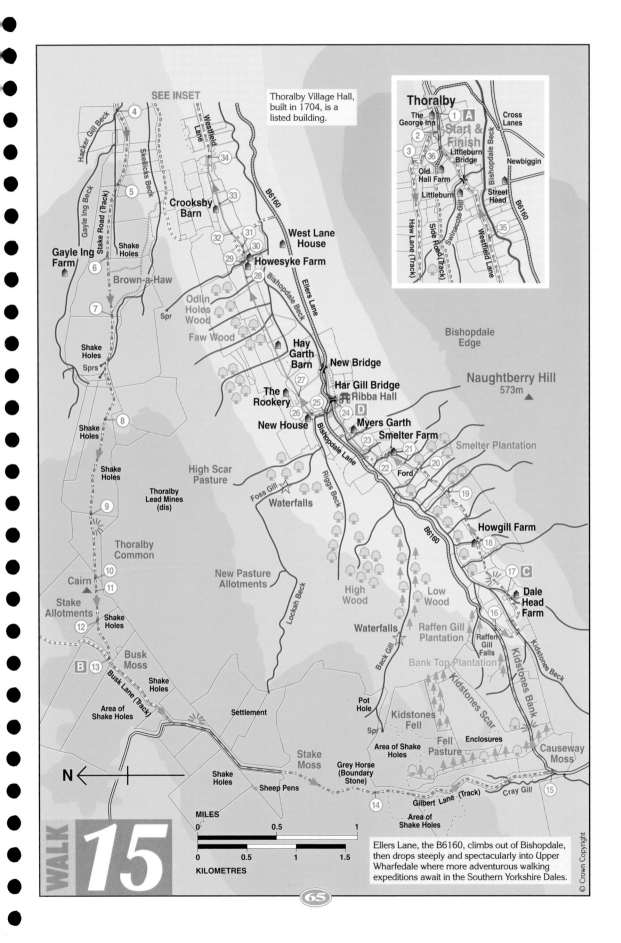

SEE INSET

Thoralby Village Hall, built in 1704, is a listed building.

Thoralby

The George Inn

① A Start & Finish

②

③ 36 Littleburn Bridge

Cross Lanes

Newbiggin

Old Hall Farm

Littleburn

Street Head

Haw Lane (Track)

Side Road (Track)

Swinacote Gill

Westfield Lane

Bishopdale Beck

35

B6160

④

Hacker Gill Beck

Westfield Lane

34

Skellicks Beck

Gayle Ing Beck

Stake Road (Track)

⑤

33

B6160

Crooksby Barn

Shake Holes

32 31

West Lane House

Gayle Ing Farm

⑥

30

29

Howesyke Farm

Brown-a-Haw

28

Bishopdale Beck

Ellers Lane

Bishopdale Edge

⑦

Odlin Holes Wood

Spr

Faw Wood

Shake Holes

Sprs

Hay Garth Barn

New Bridge

Naughtberry Hill

573m

27

Har Gill Bridge

Ribba Hall

Shake Holes

⑧

The Rookery

25 24 D

Myers Garth

Smelter Farm

Smelter Plantation

26

New House

23

21 20

Shake Holes

22 Ford

19

High Scar Pasture

Foss Gill

Bishopdale Lane

⑨

Waterfalls

Riggs Beck

B6160

Howgill Farm

Thoralby Lead Mines (dis)

18

Thoralby Common

New Pasture Allotments

High Wood

Low Wood

17 C

Cairn ⑩

⑪

16

Dale Head Farm

Stake Allotments

Lockan Beck

Waterfalls

Raffen Gill Plantation

Kidstones Beck

⑫

Shake Holes

High Wood

Raffen Gill Falls

Kidstones Scar

Busk Moss

Bank Top Plantation

B ⑬

Busk Lane (Track)

Shake Holes

Kidstones Bank

Area of Shake Holes

Settlement

Pot Hole

Kidstones Fell

Kidstones Scar

Back Gill

Spr

Enclosures

Causeway Moss

N ←

Stake Moss

Grey Horse (Boundary Stone)

Area of Shake Holes

Fell Pasture

Shake Holes

Sheep Pens

⑭

Gilbert Lane (Track)

Cray Gill

15

Area of Shake Holes

MILES
0   0.5   1

0   0.5   1   1.5
KILOMETRES

WALK 15

Ellers Lane, the B6160, climbs out of Bishopdale, then drops steeply and spectacularly into Upper Wharfedale where more adventurous walking expeditions await in the Southern Yorkshire Dales.

© Crown Copyright

Walking & Safety Tips

It is absolutely essential that anyone venturing out into the countryside, particularly hilly terrain, be correctly prepared to reduce the risk of injury or fatality. No amount of advice could cover all possible situations that may arise. Therefore the following walking and safety tips are not intended to be an exhaustive list, but merely a contribution from our personal experiences for your consideration. **We would certainly suggest that inexperienced hill walkers should never consider the routes featured in our publications** and would also advise them to initially participate in a series of guided group walks such as those arranged by various rambler groups.

Clothing & Equipment

The lists represent the basic equipment required to enjoy a full day's hill walking, reasonably safe and comfortably.
CLOTHING:- Strong, sensible footwear - preferably boots with a good sole, strong trainers/lightweight boots can be worn during prolonged dry weather, warm shirt, fibre pile jacket, warm woollen sweater, windproof/waterproof anorak with hood and leggings (several thin layers insulate more adequately than one layer), woollen gloves, woollen hat or balaclava, warm trousers (avoid denim/jeans which become very clammy and cold when wet. This could lead to exposure), and good quality woollen socks or stockings, protected by waterproof gaiters.
EQUIPMENT:- Good compass and maps of the areas, along with a survival bag, whistle or torch for implementing the International Distress Signal - 6 long blasts/flashes in quick succession followed by one minute pause then repeated (the answering signal is 3 blasts or flashes). A basic first-aid kit should also be carried, which contains - bandages, sticking plasters, safety pins, scissors and some gauze pads. Take a rucksack to carry your equipment in, and some food for a butty stop, plus some extra food for emergency rations - chocolate, fruit cake, cheese and dried fruit.

Preparation & Procedure

Ensure that yourself and the others are adequately equipped and that no-one is overburdened. Learn how to use your map and compass competently. You should always be able to at least locate yourself on a map. Find out the weather forecasts for the area. Always consider the wind chill factor - even the gentlest of winds can reduce effective temperatures to a dangerous level. Plan both the route and possible escape routes beforehand balancing terrain, weather forecast and the hours of daylight against experience whilst allowing for a safety margin. Always try to plan your walk so the prevailing wind is behind you. Always try to walk in company. It is safer and more enjoyable. Gain a basic understanding of first aid. Try to leave written details of your route, point of departure, number in your group, destination and estimated time of arrival. In an emergency this information could save a life. Maintain a steady rhythm, at the pace of the slowest walker. Take care when you are walking to avoid sprains. Be very careful where you step and remain extremely vigilant about avoiding the adder, Britain's native poisonous snake. Take regular breaks - mainly to check your progress and the next stage. Keep an eye on the weather. Always be prepared to turn back if necessary. On completion, of your journey inform the person with whom you left your written information of your safe arrival.

Stay Wise - Stay Alive

First aid on the hills requires both knowledge and common sense. If in doubt concentrate on the comfort and morale of the casualty. **IN AN EMERGENCY: STOP AND THINK - DO NOT PANIC.** If you are lost - check your surroundings carefully and try and locate yourself on your map. Find shelter and decide whether it is safe or best to use an escape route. If someone is injured, or is showing the signs of exposure - i.e. stumbling and slurred speech, shivering, irrational behaviour or collapse and unconsciousness, **STOP IMMEDIATELY,** prevent further heat loss, find shelter and place the casualty into a survival bag with extra clothing. Huddle together as a group and give the casualty some warm food and drink. **DO NOT:** rub the casualty, give alcohol, or allow further exposure. Decide then on your next course of action. Do you go for help? Or do you stay put overnight sending out the International Distress Signal? If you have to stay put overnight try and find or make adequate shelter, conserve food and drink, keep morale high, keep the casualty warm, dry and conscious, and use the International Distress Signal. If you are able to leave someone with the casualty whilst two of your party go for help from a village or farm the following information is essential; accurate location of the casualty, nature of injuries, number injured, number in group, condition of others in group (If one person is suffering it is possible that others will be too), treatment already given, and time of accident. **ALWAYS BE PREPARED FOR THE WORST** and remember that **WET + COLD = EXPOSURE.** If these conditions go unchecked, by not having the correct knowledge and equipment, then they can lead to rapid cooling of the inner body core which will, in turn, lead to exposure, the most common cause of death on the hills. **TO CONCLUDE, YOU MUST BE FULLY PREPARED AND EXPERIENCED.**